Aladdin

A Pantomime

John Crocker

Lyrics and music by
Eric Gilder

Additional numbers by
John Crocker

Samuel French — London
New York - Toronto - Hollywood

ISBN 0 573 06471 7

PRODUCTION NOTE

Pantomime, as we know it today, is a form of entertainment all on its own, derived from a number of different sources - the commedia dell'arte, (and all that that derived from), the ballet, the opera, the music hall and the realms of folk-lore and fairy tale. And elements of all of these are still to be found in it. This strange mixture has created a splendid topsy-turvy world where men are women, women are men, where the present is embraced within the past, where people are hit but not hurt, where authority is constantly flouted, where fun is poked at everything including pantomime itself at times and, above all, where magic abounds and dreams invariably come true. In other words, it is - or should be - fun. Fun to do and fun to watch and the sense of enjoyment which can be conveyed by a cast is very important to the enjoyment of the audience.

Pantomime can be very simply staged if resources are limited. Basically a tab surround at the back, tab legs at the sides and a set of traverse tabs for the frontcloth scenes, together with the simplest of small cut-out pieces to suggest the various locales - or even just placards with this information written on them - will suffice. Conversely, there is no limit to the extent to which more lavish facilities can be employed.

The directions I have given in the text adopt a middle course and are based on a permanent setting of a cyclorama skycloth at the back, a few feet in front of which is a rostrum about two feet high, running the width of the stage. About two thirds of the depth downstage is a false proscenium, immediately behind which are the lines for a set of traverse tabs. Below the false proscenium are arched entrances left and right, with possibly one foot reveals to the pro-scenium. A border will be necessary at some point between the false proscenium and the cyclorama to mask lighting battens and the top of the cyclo-rama. Lastly, there is a set of steps leading from the front of the stage into the auditorium, which I have referred to as the catwalk. I have imagined it to be set stage left, but it is unimportant whether it is left or right.

Into this permanent setting are placed various wings left and right; I have catered for one a side, set on a level with the border, but a greater depth of stage may require two a side for masking purposes. Cut-out ground-rows set on the back of the rostrum complete the full sets. On smaller stages these cut-outs seen against the cyclorama give a better impression of depth than backcloths. The frontcloth fly lines come in behind the traverse tabs. Cloths can, of course, be tumbled or rolled if flying space is limited. It is a good tip always to bring in the traverse tabs when a cloth has to be lowered, then if any hitch occurs the lights can still come up and the actors get on with the scene. Similarly, I have indicated where the traverse tabs should be closed in frontcloth scenes so that there is plenty of time for the cloth to be flown before the end of the scene. The quick flow of one scene into another is important if a smooth running production is to be achieved.

The settings and costumes should preferably be in clear bright colours to give a story book effect. Deliberate occidental touches should be introduced into some settings and some of the comics' costumes. Animal skins can be hired from Theatre-Zoo, 28 New Row, W.C.2.

Pantomime requires many props and often they will have to be home made. Instructions are given in the prop plot for any of the more awkward seeming ones. Props should also be colourfully painted and in pantomime most props should be much larger than reality. It is wise for the property master to examine carefully the practical use to which a prop is to be put - it is very painful to be hit with a Giant's club of solid wood, one of material filled with foam plastic is far gentler!

I have not attempted to give a lighting plot as this entirely depends on the equipment available, but, generally speaking, most pantomime lighting needs to be full-up, warm and bright. Pinks and ambers are probably best for this, but a circuit of blues in the cyclorama battens will help nightfall and dawn rising effects and can also provide colour variations in the backgrounds for interior scenes. Follow spots are a great help for this kind of show, but not essential. If they are available, though, it is often effective in romantic numbers to fade out the stage lighting and hold the principals in the follow spots, quickly fading up on the last few bars as this frequently helps to increase the applause! Flash boxes, with the necessary colour and flash powders, can be obtained from the usual stage electrical suppliers.

The music has been specially composed so that it is easy for the less musically accomplished to master, but it is also scored in parts for the more ambitious. If an orchestra is available well and good, but a single piano will suffice. It is an advantage, however, if there can be a drummer as well. Not only because a rhythm accompaniment enhances the numbers, but also because for some reason never yet fully fathomed slapstick hits and falls are always twice as funny if they coincide with a well timed bonk on a drum, wood-block or whatever is found to make the noise best suited to the action. A drummer can also cope with the various "whizzes" noted in the directions - a special type of whistle can be got for this - though, if necessary, they can be done off stage.

Pantomime requires a particular style of playing and production. The acting must be larger than life, but still sincere, with a good deal of sparkle and attack. Much of it must be projected directly at the audience, since one of pantomime's great advantages is that it deliberately breaks down the "fourth wall". The actors can literally and metaphorically shake hands with their audience, who become almost another member of the cast; indeed, their active participation from time to time is essential. A word of warning on this, though - the actors must always remain in control; for instance, if a villain encourages hissing he must make sure it is never to such an extent that he can no longer be heard. The producer should see that the story line is clearly brought out and treated with respect and will find an emphasis on teamwork a help here. The selfish actor continually hogging attention is distracting to the audience and very aggravating to the rest of the cast! There is always room for local gags and topical quips in pantomime, but they should not be overdone. Most important of all, the comedy, as any comedy, must never appear to be conscious of its own funniness.

Characterisation should be clear and definite. I prefer the traditional use of a man to play the Dame and a girl to play the Principal Boy. In the case of the Dame, anyway, there is a sound argument for this - audiences will laugh more readily at a man impersonating a woman involved in the mock cruelties of slapstick than at a real woman. For this reason an actor playing a Dame should never quite let us forget he is a man, while giving a sincere character performance of a woman; further, he can be as feminine as he likes, but never effeminate. Widow Twankey is an exuberant, rumbustious character, at home in any company and seldom at a loss to know how to deal with any situation.

A Principal Boy also requires a character performance, but, of course, with the implications reversed! An occasional slap of the thigh is not sufficient. Aladdin should be thought of as a cheeky young boy, full of high spirits and eager for adventure and romance.

Principal Girls can be a bore, but only if they are presented as mere pretty symbols of feminine sweetness. Princess Baldroubadour should be played as an independent minded young lady, but light hearted and certainly not without a sense of humour.

Her father, the Emperor is vague and meek, but no fool. He often uses his weaknesses to his own advantage when dealing with his spouse, the Empress. She, of course, is never in the slightest vague or meek, but always very sure of herself and overbearing.

Ping and Pong, their Police Force, leave much to be desired in the execution of their duties. Ping, though, does realise he is not very efficient, but tries to be, nevertheless. Pong does not even try - he is aware that his brain moves too slowly for efficiency.

Wishee Washee finds life a slight worry and a puzzlement. He is continually finding himself in situations neither of his choosing nor making. All the same, he usually manages to emerge more or less unscathed.

His pet Panda, Typhoo, is a lumbering, kindly, lovably greedy animal, but with a spark or two of mischief. To play this kind of animal successfully the performer must "think" the part very hard. It will be found surprising - and very rewarding - just how much can be conveyed in this way.

Abanazar is an arch villain, but not without his ridiculous side and should be played with a suspicion of a twinkle.

The Slaves of the Ring and Lamp should look as grotesque, but magnificent as possible and be played as obviously powerful, but rather remote creatures - Genii are seemingly devoid of any private life.

The Camel is as supercilious and independent as camels always are.

I have made provision for a Chorus of six, but naturally the number used will depend on the number available.

                                                                John Crocker.

CHARACTERS

PING)
)   - Pekin Police Force.
PONG)

ALADDIN

TYPHOO   - A Panda.

WISHEE WASHEE   - Widow Twankey's Laundry Boy.

THE EMPEROR OF CHINA

THE EMPRESS OF CHINA

WIDOW TWANKEY

PRINCESS BALDROUBADOUR

ABANAZAR

THE SLAVE OF THE RING

THE SLAVE OF THE LAMP

A CAMEL

CHORUS   - as Coolies, Princess's Attendants, Cave Spirits, Slave Girls, Eastern Dancers, etc.

SYNOPSIS OF SCENES

PART I

Scene 1:   THE MARKET PLACE, PEKIN.

Scene 2:   THE END OF NOWHERE & WATLING STREET, PEKIN.

Scene 3:   WIDOW TWANKEY'S LAUNDRY.

Scene 4:   OUTSIDE THE LAUNDRY.

Scene 5:   ON THE WAY TO THE CAVE.

Scene 6:   THE MAGIC CAVE OF JEWELS.

PART II

Scene 7:   WIDOW TWANKEY'S LAUNDERETTE.

Scene 8:   THE EMPEROR'S AUDIENCE CHAMBER.

Scene 9:   ABANAZAR'S DEN.

Scene 10:   ALADDIN'S PALACE.

Scene 11:   OUTSIDE THE PALACE.

Scene 12:   THE PALACE, AFRICA.

Scene 13:   LOST PROPERTY.

Scene 14:   ALADDIN'S WEDDING BANQUET.

Running time approximately two hours and thirty minutes.

PART I

Scene One - THE MARKET PLACE, PEKIN.

Full-set. Cut-out around row of Chinese shops and houses on back of
rostrum and in C., a notice with "MARKET PLACE, PEKIN" written
on it in Chinese characters, and above it a sign on which is a long-
fingernailed Chinese hand pointing off R., and the words "TO THE
HONOURABLE IMPERIAL BATH-HOUSE". At L. end of rostrum an
oriental bridge runs obliquely onstage. A set of steps leading down from
rostrum to stage is placed in front of bridge and another set is R.C., in
front of rostrum. House wing L., with practical door and practical
window and notice above door "WIDOW TWANKEY'S LAUNDRY". House
wing R., with practical door and inn ign hanging out from it - "THE
UNWORTHY CHOPSTICK & DRAGON ARMS" and underneath - "PROP.
WUN LUNG". Flower pot in front of L. side of pros. arch.

(CHORUS discovered singing and dancing OPENING CHORUS.)

MUSIC 2   "CHING-A-LING" (Words by John Crocker)

CHORUS: In Pekin City the sun shines bright,
                        Morning, morning, what a lovely morning -
                        Our hearts are gay and our steps are light,
                            Ching-a-ling, ching-a-ling-lee
                        We've left our work to take the air
                        And thrown away all strife and care.
                        Ching-a-ling, ling-ling, ching-a-ling-a-ling-a-
                                                            ling,
                        Ching-a-ling, ling, ling-a-ling-lee.

                        Our city's like a lady fair,
                        Morning, morning, what a lovely morning -
                        Bedeck'd with flowers and gems so rare,
                            Ching-a-ling, ching-a-ling-lee
                        And so there are without a doubt
                        A hundred things to sing about
                        Ching-a-ling, ling-ling, ching-a-ling-a-ling-a-
                                                            ling,
                        Ching-a-ling, ling, ling-a-ling-lee.

                        In Pekin city the sun shines bright,
                        Morning, morning, what a lovely morning,
                        Our hearts are gay and our steps are light,
                            Ching-a-ling, ching-a-ling-lee
                        We hope you will our gladness share
                        And throw away your strife and care.
                        Ching-a-ling, ling-ling, ching-a-ling-a-ling-a-
                                                            ling,
                        Ching-a-ling, ling, ling-a-ling-lee.

MUSIC 3 (EFFECT 1 Sound of police siren off R., and SERGEANT PING scoots
        from U.R., on scooter labelled "POLICE", which he propels D.C.,
        towards floats.)

CHORUS;   Look out! Stop! STOP!

(PING stops just in time at the floats, and gets off to L. of scooter.)

PING: Ah, that had you worried, didn't it? You thought I was going over, didn't you?

CHORUS: Yes.

PING: So did I. Well, good morning honourable all.

CHORUS: Good morning, Sergeant Ping.

PING: (taking out notebook) Nice day for a few crimes. Any of you lot committed any?

CHORUS: No, Sergeant.

PING: Pity. We haven't had a decent conviction in months. Never mind, I've got an announcement here forbidding everybody to do something, so perhaps that'll encourage one of you to go and do it. Listen carefully. (he bends his knees policeman-like and coughs importantly.) Ahem! Honourable Commoners, this day will her Serene Highness Princess Baldroubadour proceed in state to the Imperial Baths. His Imperial Majesty has decreed that no honourable commoner shall gaze on her save on pain of death by dishonourable chopper. Honourable commoners, you have been warned. All clear?

CHORUS: No. What's it mean?

PING: It means if you don't want your nappers napped you'd better nip off.

CHORUS: (going off L. and R.) Oh, shame. We wanted to see her. It's not fair. Why shouldn't we see her? etc.

PING: Now, no loitering. Move along there, please.

(CHORUS are gone)

Now where's the other half of the police force? Constable Pong! Constable Pong! No, no, no. Let us use the wonders of modern science. (takes hand mike from handlebar) I'll call him up on his squad scooter. (facing R.) Calling Squad scooter 34, 34, 343 oblique 34, 34 343 oblique 2. Where are you? Where are you? Over.

(EFFECT 2 Police siren off L., as PONG enters D.L. propelling a similar scooter and speaking into hand mike)

PONG: I'm here. I'm here. Over. (bumps into PING and knocks him over) Oops. Right over.

PING: You fool. Over.

PONG: Sorry. Over.

PING: Well, help me up. Over.

PONG: Certainly. Over. (he does so)

PING: Thank you. Out. (replaces hand mike)

PONG: Not at all. In. (replaces hand mike)

PING:	Out.
PONG:	In.
PING:	Out.
PONG:	In.
PING:	Out.
BOTH:	(singing)
	Jolly boating weather
	And a hay harvest -
PING:	Stop it. We're supposed to be on duty.

(They put their scooters: PING'S to R., and PONG'S to L.)

But the trouble is we haven't any duties to do. The only offence we've had lately is young Aladdin Twankey playing cricket in the streets and breaking the police station windows. It's just not bad enough. Somehow things have got to get worse.

MUSIC 4. "IN OLD PEKIN" (Words and Music by John Crocker, arr., Eric Gilder.)

PING:	Listen here, P.C. Pong,
	No one's put a foot wrong
	In the city of Old Pekin.
PONG:	Yes, I know, there just ain't
	Not one single complaint
	To be found now in Old Pekin.
BOTH:	So we haven't got a thing to do,
	Except sit here and admire the view.
PONG:	Tell you what, Sergeant Ping,
	We must put some more zing
	In the crime of Old Pekin.
PING:	Good idea, I agree
	We'll show no clemency
	To the people of Old Pekin.
BOTH:	And though 'twill seem like false pretences
	We shall invent some new offences.
PING:	We'll put narks,
PONG:	In the parks,
PING:	To report any larks -
BOTH:	To the perlice of Old Pekin.
PONG:	Make a pass,
PING:	Steal a kiss,
PONG:	And they'll soon be for this

BOTH: (continued)
> In the prison of old Pekin.
> Where they'll be fed on bread and water,
> For doing what they didn't oughter.
> So beware! Have a care!
> For we mean to ensnare.

PONG: Ev'ryo.............ne   )
PING: Ev'ryone in old Pek-i-i-i-n) (simultaneously)

(PING hits PONG with truncheon and stops his sustained note)

PING: Ev'ryone,

PONG: Ev'ryone,

BOTH: In old Pekin.

(EFFECT 3 Glass crash off L.)

PING: What's that?

PONG: Only Aladdin breaking the police station windows again.

PING: Only! After him! Quick!

(They both run towards their scooters and collide in C. and fall over)

Clumsy!

CHORUS: (off) Look out, Aladdin.

(PING rises quickly and gets on his scooter, blowing his whistle. PONG is rather more dazed and is just getting up with his back to PING as PING comes scooting over, knocks him down and continues off L. MUSIC 5. ALADDIN, followed by CHORUS runs on from L., on rostrum and down steps.

ALADDIN: This way boys and girls.

CHORUS GIRL: (sees PONG still floundering on floor) No, Aladdin. There's one of them here!

ALADDIN: This way then!

(They go to run off L. below rostrum. PING'S whistle sounds off L.)

Too late! Here comes Ping again!

(He sees PONG'S scooter, grabs it and scoots off R. on it. PING re-enters L., on his scooter just as PONG is rising again with his back to L., and knocks him down then continues off R., still blowing his whistle and shouting as he comes across)

PING: Hey, come back! Come back!

PONG: I'm getting out of this.

(He climbs up onto rostrum just as ALADDIN scoots on from R., on rostrum and knocks him down)

ALADDIN: Oops! Sorry. But thanks for the loan. (gives scooter to PONG and jumps down from rostrum) Hide me, boys and girls.

(CHORUS crowd round him in C. PING enters R., on rostrum on scooter just as PONG is about to rise again. PONG sits again hastily.)

PONG: Missed.

PING: Well, don't just sit there. Which way did he go?

PONG: I don't know.

PING: (to CHORUS) Which way did he go?

CHORUS: We don't know.

PING: You in the middle. Which way did he go?

ALADDIN: (bobbing up and crossing arms to point both ways) That-ataway. (bobs down again)

PONG: Whichaway?

PING: (crossing arms) Thisaway.

PONG: Rightaway.

(PING scoots off L., on rostrum. PONG R. CHORUS open out. ALADDIN moves down C.)

ALADDIN: Well, that's shaken them off, but I'd better remember to keep out of their way for a bit.

6th C. GIRL: Yes - they might be back here soon.

ALADDIN: What for?

6th C. GIRL: To clear the streets for Princess Baldroubadour's procession to the baths.

ALADDIN: Then I think I'll stay and see the Princess.

7th C. GIRL: You'd better not or you'll have your head chopped off.

ALADDIN: I bet you I won't. I know just the way to see her without being seen.

7th C. GIRL: How?

ALADDIN: I'm not going to tell you lot, but I'm going to do it. And what's more, I'll probably talk to her too and - if she's as beautiful as they say she is - I might fall in love with her.

(CHORUS laugh)

Oh, you can laugh, but it could happen. You wait and see.

MUSIC 6   "WHERE THERE'S LIFE"

ALADDIN: She loves me, she loves me not, she loves me, she
                                      loves me not -
                My head's completely in a whirl;
                But while there's life there's always hope

ALADDIN: (continued)

              That she might be my girl.
              Who knows? Was she sent for me? Her smile might
                                 be meant for me,
              And maybe yes and maybe no,
              But some day she may realise
              That I adore her so.
              Fate has many funny ways of keeping us apart,
              But you can keep your spirit if there's hope within
                                 your heart.
              She might be, she mightn't be, she might be, she
                                 mightn't be -
              My heart is waiting for a sign
              That some fine day she'll come to me
              And turn my blood to wine,
              And then I'll know she's mine!

(Exit ALADDIN C.R., and CHORUS variously)

WISHEE: (off U.L.) Not so fast Typhoo, wait!
MUSIC 7

(TYPHOO, a PANDA, lumbers on L. on rostrum straining at a long leash round her neck. At the other end of which she drags a puffing and panting WISHEE WASHEE)

       No, hold on a minute, Typhoo!

(She jumps down C., off rostrum so that WISHEE tumbles down after her and is pulled along on his knees towards D.R.)

       Heel, girl. Heel, I say!

(She starts to run to L., as he is stumbling to his feet again.)

       No, no, I said heel - not run!

(She stops very suddenly in C., and sits down facing front so that he continues on, trips over her legs and falls flat on his face.)

       Typhoo, I was supposed to be taking you for a walk. Help me up, please.

(TYPHOO shambles to her feet and tugs him up by the seat of his pants)

Aah! Typhoo, careful with your claws. Ooh, look, people.

(TYPHOO hastily jumps up)

(protectively) It's all right, there's no need to be bashful. I'm sure they're very nice people. I'll introduce you, if you like. How do you do? I'm Wishee Washee, Widow Twankey's laundry boy.

(TYPHOO shakes his hand)

Very pleased to meet - no, no, we know each other. I'm introducing me so that I can introduce you.

(TYPHOO runs to D.R.)

No don't run away Typhoo, there's nothing to be frightened of.

(As he turns to speak to audience TYPHOO moves onto cat walk and into audience)

WISHEE: (continued) Sorry about this but she's very shy. All pandas are, you know. It takes them a long time to -

(He sees TYPHOO in the audience shaking hands with all and sundry)

Typhoo, what are you doing? I've just been telling everybody how shy you are.

(TYPHOO nods her head to him very happily and continues shaking hands etc.)

Well, come back here and be shy then.

(TYPHOO a little reluctantly waves to audience and returns over catwalk)

As a panda you're supposed to have a very timid nature. It says so in all the books.

(TYPHOO scratches her head puzzled)

But then you haven't really turned out quite as I expected anyway. When I bought you they said you were a specially bred miniature giant panda.

(TYPHOO nods enthusiastically)

But you're not supposed to have grown any bigger than this - (indicates with his hands something about the size of a poodle) I think you eat too many bamboo shoots.

(TYPHOO, reminded of food, immediately begs)

No, no, no. I didn't mean that.

(He backs away from her. She follows still begging)

I shouldn't have said it. I haven't got any.

(TYPHOO sniffs, nods and tries to get her nose in his R. pocket)

Oh, very well. Here you are. Just one.

(He offers her one on the palm of his hand which she gobbles up eagerly, then begs for more.)

No, no, I said one.

(TYPHOO strokes him affectionately and rubs her head on his leg)

Well, two then. (gives it to her) But no more. You must have eaten a couple of bamboo forests already today. In fact, I've only got one more shoot left. I tell you what, let's plant it and see if it grows any bigger.

(TYPHOO nods enthusiastically)

But where?

(TYPHOO looks to R., then to L., sees flower pot in front of pros. arch and runs and points to it triumphantly)

WISHEE: (continued) A flower pot! Well, what a coincidence. (crosses to it, and plants bamboo shoot) There.

(They move away)

I wonder if it'll take long to grow?

(The shoot begins to grow out of the pot)

Apparently not.

(TYPHOO rushes back to the pot to try to get bamboo shoot. Music whizz. It whistles past her nose. She sits back astonished)

Wait Typhoo. It hasn't finished growing, yet. I can see I'll have to get somebody to keep an eye on it for us, or it'll be pinched. I know. We'll ask these people. (to audience) I say, would you look after our bamboo shoot? If anybody tries to take it you just shout "Bamboo", and then I'll come and stop them. Let's try it, shall we? You go over there, Typhoo.

(TYPHOO goes to R.)

Now, I'll go away and then Typhoo will pretend to take it.

(TYPHOO nods mischievously and rubs her tummy)

I said pretend, Typhoo. (to audience) As soon as she gets to the flower pot you shout "Bamboo" as loud as you can. Ready? Right. I'll go.

(He exits D.L. TYPHOO elaborately creeps over to shoot. AUDIENCE SHOUT. WISHEE pokes his head on D.L.)

Anyone shouted yet, Typhoo?

(TYPHOO gives a sort of grudging movement and moves away from shoot)

Really? Well, they'll have to do it louder than that. Try again.

(He disappears again. TYPHOO again creeps to shoot. AUDIENCE SHOUT. WISHEE pokes his head on again)

Yes, I think I heard a faint murmur of bamboo, then.

(TYPHOO nods, but not very enthusiastically and moves away from shoot)

Once more and be really vulgar this time. BELLOW YOUR GUTS OUT!

(He disappears. TYPHOO creeps over to shoot. AUDIENCE SHOUT. TYPHOO clasps her hands to her ears and hastily moves away to C., as WISHEE runs on to C.)

All right! Splendid! Now, don't forget to do that any time you see someone trying to take the bamboo shoot.

PING:)   (off L.) Make way for the Emperor and Empress.

PONG:)   Make way for the Emperor and Empress.

MUSIC 8 Chinese slow march begins.

WISHEE: Ooh, I say, Royalty.

(They break a little R. PING and PONG each bearing a large mace enter
with stately gait, over bridge and post themselves at either side of it.
PING L. and PONG R.)

PING: Illustrious citizens, prostrate yourselves before their
Imperial Majesties, our esteemed Emperor and Empress.

(WISHEE kneels with head down and then rises to bring TYPHOO down
into same position. Fanfare as EMPEROR and EMPRESS enter over
bridge, very dignified. The EMPEROR carries a scroll. PING and PONG
bow hitting them on their heads with the maces.)

EMPEROR:)
EMPRESS:)   Ow!

EMPRESS: Fools! (surveys WISHEE and TYPHOO) Is this all we have
to greet us?

EMPEROR: (looks round vaguely) Er - yes my dear.

EMPRESS: But we have a proclamation to make. We can't make it to
one miserable citizen and one piebald door mat.

TYPHOO: (looks up in outraged astonishment then begins to rise
growling menacingly) Grrr.

(WISHEE tries to restrain her. EMPEROR and PING and PONG run to
hide behind EMPRESS)

EMPEROR: Careful, my dear.

EMPRESS: Don't be feeble, Emperor. (even more menacingly to
TYPHOO) Grr to you.

(TYPHOO hastily returns to kneeling position)

(EMPEROR, PING and PONG come out of hiding)

You see a little firmness is all that's needed. Now we need more people.
Police, procure some more populace.

PING:)   Yes, your Majesty. (they bow and again hit EMPEROR
PONG:)   and EMPRESS)

EMPEROR:)
EMPRESS:)   Ow!

EMPRESS: You idiots!

PING:)   So sorry, your Majesties. Beg pardon, your Majesties.
PONG:)   A slip of the -

EMPRESS: Oh, never mind, let the matter drop.

PING:)
PONG:)   Certainly.

(PING and PONG drop the maces onto EMPEROR and EMPRESS's feet.

EMPEROR:)
EMPRESS:)   Ow!

EMPRESS: Get out of here and find some populace!

PING:)   Yes, your Majesty. At once, your Majesty. Populace!
PONG:)   Populace!

    (PING exits L., and PONG R.)

EMPRESS: Buffoons!

    (EMPEROR and EMPRESS come down steps.)

Those two creatures are still here, I see. Well, I suppose we must go through the usual formalities. Illustrious citizens, you may rise and greet us.

    (WISHEE and TYPHOO, prompted by WISHEE, rise.)

WISHEE: Thank you. Well - er - (bowing and nudging TYPHOO to make her bow) Good morning, esteemed Emperor and Empress.

EMPEROR:)   Good morning illustrious citizens.
EMPRESS:)

    (Slight pause)

WISHEE: Er - (bowing with TYPHOO) A <u>very</u> good morning, esteemed Emperor and Empress.

EMPEROR:)   (bowing) A <u>very</u> good morning illustrious citizens.
EMPRESS:)

WISHEE: In fact a very,(bowing with TYPHOO) very good morning, esteemed Emperor and Empress.

EMPEROR:)   A very,(bowing) <u>very</u> good morning, illustrious citizens.
EMPRESS:)

WISHEE: And it wouldn't be too much to say a very, very, (bowing with TYPHOO) <u>very</u> good -

EMPRESS: Yes, it would. It'll be afternoon if we carry on like this. We are agreed it is a good morning.

WISHEE: Yes, indeed. (bowing with TYPHOO) A good morning,
  este -

EMPRESS: Silence! Can't you understand plain Chinese?

WISHEE: Yesee.

EMPRESS: Then shut-uppee! And be offee! Chop-chopee!

WISHEE: At oncee!

    (He bows himself out backwards right round stage to exit to laundry. The EMPRESS opens her mouth to speak when WISHEE re-enters and bows himself backwards round to TYPHOO watched in astonishment by EMPRESS and with mild interest by EMPEROR.)

Sorry. Forgotee.

    (He and TYPHOO bow themselves out round stage and into laundry)

EMPRESS: Extraordinary. Oh, Emperor, my dear, look. There's a tender young bamboo shoot. They're delicious in butter. Go and pick it for me.

EMPEROR: Certainly, my dear.

(he crosses to flower pot. AUDIENCE SHOUT. Very scared he hurries back as WISHEE runs on)

They shouted at me.

EMPRESS: (to WISHEE) Well?

WISHEE: Oh - er - nothing. (aside to AUDIENCE) Thank you. (catching the EMPRESS's eye he hastily bows himself off backwards into the laundry)

EMPRESS: I'll get it myself.

(She crosses to shoot. AUDIENCE SHOUT. WISHEE rushes on, sees EMPRESS and dives back into laundry.)

They shouted at me.

(WISHEE re-enters from laundry bowing as, hands behind his back, he goes down to flower pot, whips a large notice "POISON" from behind his back and puts it against pot.)

WISHEE: (aside to AUDIENCE) Thank you.

EMPRESS: Eh?

(WISHEE shrugs and smiles ingratiatingly and again bows off into laundry)

(looking at notice) Perhaps I won't have it after all.

EMPEROR: Oh, do, my dear.

(EMPRESS glares at him.)

I mean - er.

(he is saved by the entry of the CHORUS herded on from L. and R. by PING and PONG.

PING:) Come on, honourable populace. Hurry along there.
PONG:) Prostrate yourselves, honourable populace.

(CHORUS prostrate themselves.)

PING: (bowing) Your Majesties. The honourable populace.

EMPRESS: They may rise.

(CHORUS do so.)

CHORUS: Thank you, esteemed Empress. (bowing) Good morning,
es -

EMPRESS: But they may not greet us. Emperor, we are ready. Read the proclamation.

EMPEROR: Yes, my dear. (clears throat nervously) Ahem! - Er, I
can't.

EMPRESS: Why not?

EMPEROR: (sadly) I never learnt to read.

EMPRESS: (taking scroll) But it's in your writing.

EMPEROR: (happily) Of course. I learnt to write.

EMPRESS: Emperor, words fail me.

EMPEROR: How splendid... I mean -

(CHORUS titter)

EMPRESS: Silence. I suppose I'll have to do it as usual. Illustrious citizens, this day has our daughter, Princess Baldroubadour been betrothed to the son of the late lamented Grand Vizier, his Highness Prince Pekoe. (slight pause) Well, I think a few cheers are indicated.

EMPEROR: (moving to pub) Yes, indeed.

EMPRESS: I said cheers, not beers, Emperor.

EMPEROR: Oh, pity.

EMPRESS: Populace, cheer.

PING: Hip - hip -

CHORUS: Hooray!

PING: Hip - hip -

CHORUS: Hooray!

PING: Hip - hip -

CHORUS: Hooray!

EMPRESS: That's better.

PONG: Hooray!

EMPRESS: Too late, my man, take it back.

PONG: Eh - ruh.

EMPRESS: Thank you. Now perhaps some liquid refreshment would be welcome. You may buy me a small port and lemon, Emperor.

EMPEROR: Yes, my dear, of course, only I haven't any money. I was hoping that you - ?

EMPRESS: Certainly not. Police, levy a tax immediately -

(CHORUS hastily bow themselves off backwards L. and R.)

EMPRESS: Unfortunate. You'll have to levy it on yourselves. (prods POLICE towards pub)

PING:)
PONG:) (resignedly) Yes, your Majesty. (they exit into pub)

EMPRESS: Come, Emperor.

EMPEROR: Yes, my dear.

(They too exit into pub. EFFECTS 4 & 5. Sound of motor engine back-firing (pistol), violent tooting, EFFECT 6, big crash and screams heard off R. Some CHORUS run on R. , and run off L.)

TWANKEY: (off R.) Look out! Look out!

MUSIC 9

(EFFECTS 7 and 8. More motor engine and backfiring and TWANKEY enters R. , apparently dragged on by an old chair pram labelled "WIDOW TWANKEY'S LAUNDRY DOOR TO DOOR DELIVERY SERVICE". It has a mock motor on the back and a pile of washing on the seat. She is tooting a hooter on the handle.)

It's got the better of me! I can't stop! I can't stop!

(she exits L. EFFECT 9 A loud crash off L. and shrieks from TWANKEY. She re-enters L.)

Oh, dear, oh dear, I'm sure there must be some other way to stop it. It's so inconvenient having to find a brick wall every time.

(pram trundles on and butts her in rear)

Ouch! How dare you! Get back to your garage.

(pram trundles off (pulled off by line attached to it))

Ooh that machine. It's been too big for its tyres ever since I took it on the M1.

(pram trundles on and hits her again)

Stop it! You'll ruin my reverse gear. Go away!

(pram trundles off)

Well, it is nice to see you all. How are you? Eh? Yes, I'm a bit off too. I expect it's the weather. I'm Widow Twankey by the way. And have you met our Chinese band? The one in the middle with the single chopstick is - (conductor's name)

(CONDUCTOR turns and bows to AUDIENCE)

That's it, give a little Chinese bow, dear. Ooh, I say, what a lovely bamboo shoot. Now that would make a tasty little horses-whatsit for my supper. Wait a minute, though. Poison. Oh, well, I don't mind a touch of indigestion. I always keep my Rennies handy. I'm going to pick it.

(Goes over to flower pot. AUDIENCE SHOUT)

No, no, nark it. Someone'll hear you.

(WISHEE runs on from laundry bowing madly.)

Whatever's the matter with you, Wishee?

WISHEE: (stopping rather foolishly) Oh - Mrs Twankey - I - er I was just doing my exercises.

TWANKEY: I thought your braces had got caught up with your shoe laces.

WISHEE: I say, you weren't trying to take my bamboo shoot, were you? That's for my panda.

TWANKEY: But you can't give her that. It's poison.

WISHEE: (throwing notice off) Oh, I only put that there to stop the Empress taking it.

TWANKEY: Well, I'm sure it'll make a lovely treat for dear little Mazawattee.

WISHEE: Mazawattee?

TWANKEY: I mean Quick Brew.

WISHEE: Quick Brew?

TWANKEY: Ninety-nine.

BOTH: TYPHOO! (they shake hands)

(Exit WISHEE into laundry)

TWANKEY: He's a nice boy that. A great help to me, too. I wish that son of mine, Aladdin, was more like him. But he doesn't seem to fancy work, somehow. He got that from his father, of course. He never took to it either. Ah, but there was a man, I can tell you. Well, he wasn't much really, but he was all mine. (snuffling) Oh yes, them was the days. Now where's me hanky got to? Oh, I know.

(She starts to lift up her many petticoats to get it from her red flannel knickers, then looks up at audience in a suspicious way and opens up umbrella to cover herself, removes hanky and blows nose hard, accompanied by peculiar noise from orchestra.)

Nasty touch of guitar. But still, I've a lot to be thankful for. I mean, I've kept me health and I've kept me looks - they've not kept very well, I know but then I suppose they always were a bit off. Still, there's no point in grumbling, is there?

MUSIC 10 "SIXTY GLORIOUS YEARS"

TWANKEY: Thirty glorious years, dears,
Thirty glorious years.
When you possess a figure like mine
It mellows with age, like any good wine.
I've been a vintage that's divine
For forty glorious years.

(spoken) Oh there, I've let it out! I said forty. It is forty really, of course.

Forty glorious years, dears,
Forty glorious years.
Take a day off when your birthday is here,
When mine comes around I take off a year!
So I've had nothing much to fear
For fifty glorious years.

TWANKEY: (continued - spoken) Did I hear myself say fifty? Fifty??
Oh, well...

> Fifty glorious years, dears,
> Fifty glorious years.
> Sing as you go, and life'll be fun,
> A full house until the end of the run.
> I wouldn't have missed a single one
> Of sixty - I mean, fifty - forty - thirty!

(pram trundles on - now with ALADDIN concealed in washing - and buffets her.)

> So now you're a lie detector. Oh well -
> Of sixty glorious years!

(TWANKEY goes into laundry. Enter PING and PONG over bridge.)

PING:)   Make way for her Serene Highness the Princess Baldrouba-
PONG:)   dour! Clear the streets! Clear the streets and make way!

(CHORUS enter over bridge singing. 1st CHORUS GIRL carries a cushion with a large sponge on it; 2nd CHORUS GIRL, a cushion with a loofah; 3rd CHORUS GIRL, a large bath towel and a salver with a large tablet of soap and tin of talcum powder, 4th CHORUS GIRL, a perfume spray on a salver. They process round stage as PRINCESS BALDROUBADOUR enters over bridge with 5th and 6th CHORUS GIRLS, who hold a canopy over her.

MUSIC 11 "MAKE WAY"

PING, PONG   Make way, oh make way
& CHORUS: For the Royal sponge,
> Make way, oh make way
> For the Royal Loofah,
> For towel, soap and talcum and the perfume spray -
> Make way, make way, make way, it's the Royal bath
> > day
> Make way for our lovely Princess
> All the streets must be quite clear
> > So make way.
> She is the fairest maid in China,
> None may see her passing by
> > So don't stay.

(PING, PONG and 1st, 2nd, 3rd and 4th CHORUS GIRLS exit D.R.)

5th C. GIRL: Does your Highness wish to rest awhile?

PRINCESS B: Yes. So Hi, alone. So run along both of you. Just for once I want to feel quite free.

6th C. GIRL: But, your Highness, your father -

PRINCESS B: Yes, I know it's forbidden, So Lo, but never mind. I will be responsible if anything happens, so please go.

(5th and 6th CHORUS GIRLS exit D.R. with canopy.)

PRINCESS B: (continued) But nothing will happen - it never does to a Princess. Oh, yes it does. I am to be married to Prince Pekoe, but I don't want that to happen. I want to marry someone I love. (looking round) Now what is that I wonder? (moves over to pram)

(The pile of washing on the pram begins to move and a sheet is gradually thrust aside to reveal ALADDIN.)

I do believe something is going to happen after all - I hope it isn't anything unpleasant. Oh no, rather pleasant. Who or what are you?

ALADDIN: My name is Aladdin, my lady - er - your Highness. I'm sorry if I address you wrongly, but I am not used to the ways of courts. As to what I am, well, I'm one of your subjects who's rather cramped at the moment.

PRINCESS B: Then you'd better stretch your legs.

ALADDIN: (getting out) Thank you, Princess.

PRINCESS B: What were you doing there? Were you there as a punishment?

ALADDIN: No, not for punishment, but for pleasure. I had hidden there to see you pass by. I meant only to see - not to be seen, and then - then -

PRINCESS B: And then?

ALADDIN: You looked so beautiful that I wanted to see you really well.

PRINCESS B: You may not be used to the ways of courts, Aladdin, but you say the nicest things. But isn't it very dangerous for you to be here with me?

ALADDIN: Yes, I might very well lose my head for it. But what does my head matter, when I have already lost my heart?

MUSIC 12 "HAS ANYBODY SEEN MY HEART"

> Bang, bang, bang, went my pulses
> The moment that we met
> Then my heart went out completely
> And I haven't found it yet!
>
> Has anybody seen my heart, my heart?
> My heart has been mislaid.
> It rather looks as though my heart, my heart
> Is stolen, lost or strayed.
> I'm sure I had it yesterday,
> And somehow it got free;
> But if you should be the one to find my heart,
> Then keep it safe for me.
>
> It's gone in its entirety,
> And hasn't left a clue,
> But if anyone should find my heart, my heart,
> I hope it will be you.

(Enter EMPEROR and EMPRESS from pub.)

EMPRESS: Ah, most refreshing, Emperor.

EMPEROR: I'm glad you enjoyed it, my dear. Oh, here's our daughter, with a commoner!

EMPRESS: So she is. (takes on ALADDIN) A commoner! Looking at her! Talking to her!! Holding her in his arms!!! SOMEBODY DO SOME-THING!!! Summon the guard! Fetch the Police!

EMPEROR: Call out the fire brigade.

EMPRESS: Don't be absurd. Police!! Police!!

(PING and PONG run on from pub with manacle chains. CHORUS enter from L. and R. WISHEE WASHEE and TYPHOO run out from laundry.)

WISHEE: (calling back into laundry) Widow Twankey! Widow Twankey!

(General excited buzz from all on stage.)

EMPRESS: Police, seize that man!

(TWANKEY runs on from laundry as PING and PONG are chaining ALADDIN to themselves.)

TWANKEY: Now then, what's all this todoment? Oh, Crikey!

(TWANKEY faints into WISHEE's arms. He promptly falls down with her and TYPHOO stands them both up again.)

EMPRESS: Miserable youth! For this he will forfeit his head! Won't he, Emperor?

EMPEROR: Well, I -

ALADDIN: (kneeling) Mercy, Sire! Mercy, most mighty Emperor.

EMPRESS: Mercy? No! He shall be instantly executed! Shan't he, Emperor?

EMPEROR: Well, I -

PRINCESS B: (kneeling) Oh, no, father, no, I beg of you! On my knees I beg of you!

EMPRESS: Silence child! The youth is a commoner and must die. Mustn't he, Emperor?

EMPEROR: Well, I -

TWANKEY: (grovelling) Oh Emperor, spare him! He's me only son! Spare him!

EMPRESS: Enough! Your Emperor has spoken.

EMPEROR: Have I? Oh, well -

MUSIC 13. "CANTATA" (Words and Music by John Crocker, arr., Eric Gilder)
>
> I have spoken, it has to be,
> He disobeyed my royal decree.

PRINCESS B:	But since the youth does now relent, Pray tell us, sire, your anger's spent.
EMPRESS:	Too late. Too late.
EMPEROR:	'Tis useless to solicitate.
PRINCESS B:	But wait. But wait. And soon your fury may abate.
PRINCIPALS:) CHORUS:)	So wait.
EMPRESS:	Too late.
PRINCIPALS:) CHORUS:)	Oh wait.
EMPRESS:	Too late.
EMPEROR:	The boy must be decapitate.
PING:) PONG:)	We lead him in chains off to the chop-shop.
TWANKEY:	Oh, Emperor, please, I beg you, stop, stop! He is my son, my only one.
WISHEE:	I think she means he hasn't a brother.
EMPRESS:	(spoken) Clot! Of course she means there isn't another.
EMPEROR:	In spite of all that, a peeping Tom-Tom, His head from his bod must be cut from-from.
PRINCIPALS:) CHORUS:)	No, no. No, no. Not so. Not so.
PRINCESS B:	Please let Aladdin go.
EMPRESS:	(spoken) No.
EMPEROR:	I have spoken, it has to be, He can't escape the penalty.
PRINCIPALS:) CHORUS:)	(kneeling) On bended knees we still do plead In hopes that he may yet be freed.
EMPEROR:	Cease thy pleading, for I have spoke, And will not e'er my word revoke. Come Ping, Come Pong, bring him along,) And we will right this grievous wrong.)
ALADDIN:	I've done no wrong. I've done no wrong.) (simul-) taneously)
PRINCIPALS:) CHORUS:)	He's done no wrong. He's done no wrong.)

(lights fade as ALADDIN is led off by PING and PONG, preceded by
EMPEROR, over bridge, until BLACKOUT is reached.
Close traverse tabs. Fly in Scene Two Frontcloth.)

Scene Two - THE END OF NOWHERE AND
<u>WATLING STREET</u> (or wherever is locally
appropriate), PEKIN.

(TABS to open in blackout. Set R. - a covered crystal, Set C. - a casket
containing the ring. <u>MUSIC 14.</u> <u>EFFECT 10.</u> Thunder roll and lightning,
green flash L., as ABANAZAR enters L., and is picked up by green spot.)

ABANAZAR: Let thunder roll and lightning flash -
                             I care not for their mighty crash!

(EFFECT 11. More thunder and lightning)

                             The wizard Abanazar, I,
                             In magic books I delve and pry,
                             Thus did I learn where I might trace
                             A potent charm - and here's the place!

(Finds casket)

                             A box! Is this the magic thing?
                             Stay - what's inside? (opens box) Why 'tis a ring!
                             But how to loose its secret, eh?
                             That must I learn without delay.
                             Mayhap some words engraved lie,
                             Hidden by dust from sight of eye.
                             I'll clean it up till it doth shine.

(Rubs ring with sleeve. Cymbal roll and crash, red flash C., <u>MUSIC 15,</u> as
SLAVE OF RING enters through C. of tabs and is picked up by red spot.)

                             Ten thousand joys! The secret's mine!

S. OF RING: (making salaam) Master, most dread, most august
                                                   sire,
                             Command thy slave what dost desire.
                             For whosoever wears the ring
                             Him will I serve in ev'rything. (salaams)

ABANAZAR: In ev'rything? Then art thou he
                             Whom I've sought long o'er land and sea,
                             One whose power is limitless?

S. OF RING: Nay, sire, there is - I must confess -
                             A genie mightier than I;
                             Could pluck the stars from out the sky,
                             Could mountains move, could drain the seas,
                             And other wonders like to these
                             Could he perform.

ABANAZAR: 'Tis he I seek!
                             Tell me where - in what hidden creek -
                             Can this rare prodigy be found?

S. OF RING: I know not, master most renown'd.

ABANAZAR: Tcha!

S. OF RING: (moving L.) But here in this corner lies
A crystal with all-seeing eyes.

(SLAVE removes cover from crystal. ABANAZAR crosses and bends over it, making passes with his hands.) <u>MUSIC 16.</u>

ABANAZAR: Abracadabra! Abracadee!
Show me that which I would see!

Good, good, my genie. All's shown here.
First in view doth a lamp appear.
It holds in thrall the wond'rous slave,
But, 'tis hid in a magic cave -
In far off China, more's the pity -
Situate near Pekin city.
But hold! What's this that is reveal'd?
The lamp is curst! The cave is seal'd!
And only one can break the spell,
A youth, who does in Pekin dwell.
His name? Aye, in the restless swarm
From wreathing smoke the letters form -
Aladdin, eh! Aladdin, so!
I must to Pekin straightway go.
Could'st thou, slave, quickly take me there?

S. OF RING: In but a moment through the air.

ABANAZAR: Come, then, my djin, let's haste away!

S. OF RING: Master, I hear and I obey.

(He salaams. Cymbal crash, **EFFECT 12, thunder roll**, simultaneously with red flash and BLACKOUT. Music whizz. Tabs open to reveal Chinese street cloth, appropriately named. (If a cloth is not used, open tabs to reveal a flat suitably painted. A 6-foot would do.) Lights up.)

Behold we are in Pekin, sire.

ABANAZAR: We are? Such swiftness I admire.
As swiftly young Aladdin find -
No, stay - first I must turn my mind
To how to bend his will to mine.
I have it - yes! His uncle - fine!
I'll be his rich, but long-lost nunky,
Go fetch him hence, my magic flunkey.

S. OF RING: Master, I hear and I obey.

(Makes pass. FLICKER LIGHTS, THREE MUSIC WHIZZES. ALADDIN, still chained to PING and PONG, lands with them on R. of stage, in front of S. of RING as if they had been thrown down. All look rather dazed.)

PING: Hey, leggo! Put us down, I say.

(S. OF RING salaams to ABANAZAR who indicates to him to go. Exit S. of RING)

ABANAZAR: (crossing to them) Gentlemen, let me help you up. I fear you must have tripped.

PING: Tripped! Oh yes, we've had a trip all right - all the way from the execution shed.

(They rise.)

ALADDIN: Well, personally, I'd much rather be here.

PING: Yes, Aladdin, I daresay you would.

ABANAZAR: Aladdin! Not Aladdin Twankey?

ALADDIN: Yes, that's me.

ABANAZAR: My boy, come to your uncle's arms.

ALADDIN: Uncle's?

ABANAZAR: Yes, yes - I am your dear father's long lost brother.

ALADDIN: But he didn't have a brother.

ABANAZAR: Don't tell me he never mentions me - his own brother Abanazar?

ALADDIN: Well, no, I'm afraid he doesn't. You see, he's been dead for some years now.

ABANAZAR: Dead? Dead! And never called me brother! Ten thousand sorrows! I have returned too late to share my riches with him. Never mind, my boy, I shall share them with you. Allah be praised that I have found you.

PING: Well, I'm afraid you're going to lose him now, 'cos we've got to take him back to the block to be deblocked.

ABANAZAR: You mean, he is to be executed?

PONG: No. He's going to have his head chopped off.

ABANAZAR: Alas! What a miserable homecoming is mine.

(Enter EMPRESS R., unseen by others)

If you were not such upright, honest-looking fellows, I would bribe you to let my nephew escape, but I see it would be useless.

PING: Yes, useless. How much?

ABANAZAR: A hundred pieces of gold.

PING: A hund -

ABANAZAR: Each, of course.

PING: Lummee! We'd let a whole prison-full escape for that, wouldn't we?

PONG: Er - no.

PING: Yes, you fool.

PONG: (lifting helmet with free hand so that PING can hit him with his truncheon) Yes, you fool.

ABANAZAR: Then if you will release Aladdin now, I think you will find the right amount there. (produces two bags from his sleeves)

EMPRESS: (intervening and taking bags) Yes, I'm sure I shall. The charge for unsuccessful escapes is the same as for successful ones. Come, my incorruptible police force.

PING:)
PONG:)   Yes, esteemed Empress.

ABANAZAR: The Empress! Madam, had I known I must deal with you I should not have offered such a paltry sum. But, if you will accept a gift of one hundred mules laden with as much gold as they can carry, they shall be at your palace gates instantly.

EMPRESS: Thank you, I accept the gift. And now, I'm afraid we must carry on with the execution.

ABANAZAR: But madam, the boy is my only nephew whom I found but a moment since after many weary years of searching.

EMPRESS: Dear me - how sad. But you will excuse us I know. Our execution was rather held up by the prisoner and his escort disappearing suddenly -

ABANAZAR: Empress - do you refuse to release the boy?

EMPRESS: That is what I've been trying to indicate.

ABANAZAR: I warn you - you do so at your peril.

EMPRESS: At my peril - Pshaw! Come enough of this trifling!

ABANAZAR: Aye, enough!

(ABANAZAR makes a magic pass. Green flash. **EFFECT 13, thunder roll** and BLACKOUT. Lights up. ALADDIN and ABANAZAR have disappeared. ABANAZAR's fiendish laugh is heard off. EMPRESS is now chained to PING and PONG, who appear to be transfixed.)

EMPRESS: Sudden thunderstorm for the time of year - Aaahh! They've escaped! After them!

(Close traverse tabs slowly and fly-out cloth during following. PING and PONG come to life. PING runs R. and tugs the other two with him, then PONG runs L., tugging the other two.)

No, not that way - this way.

(They run R. again)

No, the other way.

(PONG runs round in front of EMPRESS to R. and PING, under PONG and EMPRESS's attached arms, runs round in front of EMPRESS to L. If the length of the chains allow them to get round a second time, so much the better. They rotate in this tight bunch.)

EMPRESS: (continued) Get a blacksmith! Get me out of these things!

<u>MUSIC 17</u>.

    (They rotate to exit R., as - BLACKOUT.)

    (Open traverse tabs.)

Scene Three - WIDOW TWANKEY'S
LAUNDRY

(Full set. Set on front of rostrum: - R. C. , cut-out of grandfather
clock with practical door; C. , small flat with comic Chinese wall telephone and framed pictures; L. C. , cut-out cupboard with practical door,
small shopping bag and TYPHOO's lead on door. Wing L. with practical
sash. Rug in front of opening D. L. Wing R. with kitchen range in front
of it. Plate rack above range, with prop plates. Prop poker, with red-
painted end, on range. Large bucket set downstage of range. Table C. ,
with chair R. of it and small footstool in front of it. Cloth on table.
Basket of laundry set D. R.)

(MUSIC 18. Enter TYPHOO from opening D. R. She looks round carefully
then tiptoes U. R. and looks off above wing; tiptoes to L. and looks through
window; tiptoes D. L. and looks off. She nods satisfied, and creeps down
to bamboo shoot and rubs her tummy.)

(AUDIENCE SHOUT. TYPHOO tries to hush them and suddenly WISHEE
pops up just in front of her at L. end of orchestra pit.)

WISHEE: Now, now, Typhoo.

(TYPHOO, horror-struck, scuttles away and tries to hide by plunging
head under clothes in laundry basket.)

(Turning to AUDIENCE) Thank you so much. You're looking after my
bamboo shoot very well. Now I'll just nip up on top.

(He starts to do so and falls back. Terrible bangings and crashings in
pit, and shouts from WISHEE.)

(TYPHOO looks up startled, with a pair of ladies bloomers on her head
and runs down to floats to see what has befallen WISHEE.)

(WISHEE emerges with a broken drum round his neck.) I say, I'm
terribly sorry. But what a bit of luck it was only one of your little drums.
(takes it off and hands it to drummer) Well - er - goodbye, thank you
for having me. (he scrambles up onto stage with help from TYPHOO)
Oh - er - your triangle, I think.

(Hands to drummer a very bent triangle which has got caught on one of his
coat buttons. A crash in the orchestra as of a triangle being thrown down.)

(to TYPHOO) You know, I don't think that drummer likes me.

(TYPHOO shakes her head and strokes him consolingly.)

(WISHEE notices that he has a tambourine round his ankle; looks to see
whether drummer is looking and motions to TYPHOO to pull it off. This
she does and he lands with a crash. While he is getting up she starts to
play tambourine, he grabs it hastily from her and hides it behind his back,
smiles ingratiatingly at drummer and moves over and flings it off D. L.
Then he and TYPHOO run to R. , putting their fingers in ears to avoid
hearing crash. EFFECT 14. Tambourine crash off L. and a cry from
TWANKEY and she appears D. L. rubbing her head.)

TWANKEY: Well, really, as if I haven't enough to worry about without

TWANKEY: (continued) people throwing tambourines at me.

(WISHEE tries to shush her. She moves in and trips over rug)

Drat that rug. (smooths it out and crosses R., in front of table) If I've told Aladdin once I've told him a hundred times not to scuffle it up. (falls flat on footstool) And he's moved that footstool out again. He is a naughty boy. I'll box his ears for him when I catch him.

(TYPHOO and WISHEE help her up)

What am I saying? Box his ears indeed, when for all I know I may never see the poor lamb again. (she bursts into tears)

(WISHEE and TYPHOO console her)

WISHEE: There, there, Mrs Twankey. (looking for hanky in his pockets) Don't cry. Where's my hanky? (sees bloomers on TYPHOO's head and takes them) Never mind, these'll do. Now dry your eyes and have a good blow.

(He dabs her eyes with the bloomers and holds them for her to blow her nose. She does so. Noise from orchestra)

Oh dear, I think you've gone a bit too far. (turns bloomers round and displays large hole. Rips them in two. (two halves joined by numerous poppers)) Never mind. We can charge as two dusters. (he throws them into basket and puts it D.L.) Now you sit down, Mrs T. I'm sure every-thing's going to be all right. Isn't it, Typhoo?

(TWANKEY sits.)

(TYPHOO nods.)

TWANKEY: But what if they do what they said they'd do to him? He'll never be the same again without his head. (dissolves into fresh tears)

WISHEE: You mustn't take on so, Mrs Twankey. (beginning to get tearful himself) I'll make you a nice cup of tea.

TWANKEY: (still tearful) You can't.

WISHEE: (tearful) Why not?

TWANKEY: I've forgotten to buy any. (lets out a howl)

WISHEE: Well, never mind, I'll nip out and get some. (also lets out a howl then stops) What am I crying for? (moves U.R. and gets down very small shopping bag and TYPHOO's lead from cupboard door) Would you like a little walk, Typhoo?

(TYPHOO jumps up immediately and runs across and bolts off D.R.)

Oi, come back! You're not dressed yet.

(TYPHOO returns to have her lead put on. She is a little impatient about it.)

Is there anything else you want while I'm out?

TWANKEY: No, I don't think so, dear. Oh yes. Could you get a pound of sausages?

WISHEE: (turning to go) Right.

(TYPHOO runs off and we see her lead stretched taut.)

TWANKEY: Oh, and three pounds of flour, four of potatoes, a packet of cornflakes, a jar of strawberry jam, a jar of marmalade, two halves of butter, one of marge and while you're about it a nice bit of cheese.

(WISHEE looks with increasing dubiety at his little shopping bag. At the same time having a sort of tug of war not to be pulled off.)

Also a bottle of piccalilli, a dozen eggs, a pound of caster, pound of gran, pound of lump, pound of dem, two tins of pineapple chunks and - Oh well I'll do the big shop tomorrow.

WISHEE: You will? (he relaxes for a second and is yanked through door)

TWANKEY: Oh and - . Oh, he's gone. Never mind. I must have a few things in in case that naughty Aladdin turns up again. Oh, if only I could have him back now I swear I'd never lift a finger against him for the rest of me natural not if he was ever so.

(ALADDIN runs in D.L., followed by ABANAZAR.)

ALADDIN: Mother, I've escaped!

TWANKEY: Yes, dear. Wipe your feet and don't scuffle up the rug. Ah, yes, if only he was here now.

ALADDIN: But, mother, don't you understand? I've escaped!

TWANKEY: Yes, all right, dear. Don't keep on about it. You've escaped - you've escaped? (turns) ALADDIN!

(Rushes to ALADDIN, falling over footstool. ALADDIN helps her up.)

(kissing him) Oh, my boy, my dear, dear boy! (slapping him) You naughty little tyke you. (kissing him) I'm so pleased to see you. (slapping him) You little imp you. (leading him across to R.) Now, come on - come and sit down, dear. (almost presses him onto stove) No, not there, that's the stove - (pushing him onto chair) Try the chair, it's cooler. That's it. (sitting on stove) Now, tell me all about - Aaahhh!! (jumps up, clutching bottom, and sits in bucket, but can't get out again. Propels herself downstage still in it then rises, bent double by it) I can't get the dratted thing off!

ABANAZAR: (moving to help her) Allow me.

(ABANAZAR pulls bucket off, TWANKEY falls onto her face. ABANAZAR puts bucket D.L.)

TWANKEY: Oh, thank you, my boy. (almost kisses ABANAZAR) Ow! You're not my boy, are you? Oh I say, nearly kissed a strange man. (to ALADDIN) Who is it, dear?

ALADDIN: It's the gentleman who helped me to escape.

TWANKEY: (vigorously pumping ABANAZAR by hand) Oh, my dear Mr Whatever-your-name-is, how can we ever thank you enough? (nearly

TWANKEY: (continued) kisses him again) Oops, nearly did it again.

ALADDIN: And, mother, he's my uncle.

TWANKEY: Is he? Well, in that case, it's all right then. (forces
ABANAZAR back over her knee, then suddenly drops him) What are you
talking about? You haven't got an uncle.

ABANAZAR: Don't say you have forgotten me too? Your dear husband's
long lost brother.

TWANKEY: Then you must have been lost a very long time indeed
because I've never heard of you, Mr er, Mr - er -

ABANAZAR: Abanazar.

TWANKEY: Well, I don't mind if I do.

ABANAZAR: Do what?

TWANKEY: 'Ave a banana.

ABANAZAR: No, no - Ababana - Tcha! Abanazar.

TWANKEY: Oh no, I'm quite sure we never had any of them in the
family. We had the measles and the whooping cough and the Scarlatina...

ABANAZAR: But why else should I have returned to the scene of my
youth, to share with my brother's family all my wealth?

TWANKEY: Wealth? Well, I rather think I do remember you now, Mr -
er, Mr - er - Abatomato. Oh, yes, of course - dear old Abey. (shaking
hands with him again) Well, it is nice to see you again, Abey. Come and
sit down, Abey. (pulls him up from floor) Aladdin, a chair for your
uncle Abey.

(ALADDIN vacates chair and moves U.C. TWANKEY puts ABANAZAR
into chair)

(on ABANAZAR's R.) Have you come far?

ABANAZAR: From Africa.

TWANKEY: Really? Well, that is a tidy step, isn't it? I expect you'd
like a bite to eat. (moving R.)

ABANAZAR: Thank you, dear sister-in-law, but I fear we must be
going very soon.

TWANKEY: Going? Whatever for?

ABANAZAR: I think it would be wise for my dear nephew to disappear
for a few days.

ALADDIN: Uncle's right, mother. (looking out of window and then
moving down) In fact, the police might be here any minute now looking for
me.

ABANAZAR: And it happens to fit in with a little plan of mine. There is
a small task I wish Aladdin to perform for me; it necessitates a journey
to the mountains, but if he will do me this favour I promise he will return
a rich man.

TWANKEY: You must go rightaway, Aladdin. I expect you'd like a
little drop of something for the road though first (nudging him), eh, Abey?

ABANAZAR: Well, er -

TWANKEY: Come along then.

   (EFFECT 15. Knock off D.L.)

See who it is, dear. And if it's the police come to fetch you - tell 'em
you're not here. Come on, Abey.

(Exit D.R., with ABANAZAR. PRINCESS BALDROUBADOUR looks on
D.L. disguised by veil.)

PRINCESS B: May I come in?

ALADDIN: Oh, good day, miss. Yes, come in.

   (PRINCESS BALDROUBADOUR enters.)

What can I do for you?

PRINCESS B: Well, you can ask me to sit down.

ALADDIN: Very well. Please sit down. (PRINCESS sits) Anything else?

PRINCESS B: Yes, you can kiss me.

ALADDIN: And suppose I don't care to?

PRINCESS B: Why, then I suppose I shan't be kissed. But I don't see why
you won't. (removes veil)

ALADDIN: Princess!

PRINCESS B: Poor Aladdin. I had to disguise myself to get away from
the Palace, and then I couldn't resist teasing you. I came to warn you that
father and the Police are coming here to search for you.

ALADDIN: How soon will they be here?

PRINCESS B: Not for a little while yet. Where will you hide?

ALADDIN: Up in the mountains. An uncle of mine is taking me there.
It was he who helped me to escape, and do you know, he says he's going to
make me a rich man so perhaps all our dreams will come true after all.

MUSIC 19. "LET'S GO DREAMING"

> Let's go dreaming wide awake,
>   Let's pretend it's real.
> Let's imagine we can do
>   Exactly as we feel.
> Let's build castles in the air,
>   Let's imagine bliss.
> Let's pretend that every hour
>   Is just as fine as this
> Sleeping dreams may worry you,
> Make you ill at ease.
> But if you dream while wide awake
> You shape them as you please.

ALADDIN: (continued)
So let's go dreaming you love me,
As much as I love you.
And if we dream it hard enough
Our daydreams may come true.

(PRINCESS BALDROUBADOUR exits D.L., throwing kiss to ALADDIN. TWANKEY and ABANAZAR enter D.R. TWANKEY has a feather duster.)

ABANAZAR: A most excellent beverage, dear sister-in-law. What is the name of that rare nectar?

TWANKEY: Guinness. Who was that just now, Aladdin?

ALADDIN: Oh - er - just somebody from the Palace.

TWANKEY: From the Palace! (crossing to ALADDIN) Then the sooner you're off the better. (kissing him) Goodbye, my dear boy, behave yourself and do whatever your uncle says.

ALADDIN: I will, mother.

TWANKEY: (kissing him again) That's a good boy. Goodbye, Abey -

(TWANKEY is about to bid ABANAZAR a fond farewell when a loud knocking starts off D.L. EFFECT 16.)

PING: (off D.L.) Open in the name of the Emperor!

TWANKEY: Crikey! They're here! Out the back way!

(TWANKEY, ALADDIN and ABANAZAR run to exit above R. wing. As they arrive heavy knocking starts. EFFECT 17.)

PONG: (off U.R.) Open in the name of the er - the er - the Emperor!

TWANKEY: Too late! Through the scullery!

(They run to opening D.R., as they arrive loud knocking starts off D.R. EFFECT 18.)

EMPRESS: (off D.R.) Open in the name of the Emperor!

ALADDIN: (they turn back) We must hide. Quickly, under the table!

(ABANAZAR and ALADDIN run upstage and start to get under table on upstage side. TWANKEY dithers for a moment or two then starts to get under table on downstage side.)

Not you, mother! You must get rid of them somehow.

(TWANKEY rises. EFFECT 19. Knocking D.L.)

PING: (off) Open up at once!

TWANKEY: (running D.L.) Yes, all right, all right.

PONG: (off. EFFECT 20. Knocking) Open the door!

TWANKEY: (running U.R.) On me way!

EMPRESS: (off. EFFECT 21. Knocking) Open this door instantly!

TWANKEY: (running D.R.) Coming! Coming!

PING: (off. EFFECT 22. Knocking) Open, or we'll break the door down!

TWANKEY: (running D.L.) Shan't be a jiffy.

(EFFECT 23. Telephone rings. She starts running to it.)

That's all I wanted.

(As she passes window, EMPEROR knocks on it. She opens window.)

Well?

EMPEROR: (poking head in) We want to come in.

TWANKEY: I know! (slams window shut, catching EMPEROR's head and runs on.)

EMPEROR: Ow!

TWANKEY: (running back) Sorry. (she pulls window up, pushes his head away and shuts window again and runs to phone and lifts receiver.) Hello?

VOICE: (miked if possible) Hello. This is a wrong number. Goodbye

TWANKEY: Goodbye. (click on line. She does take on receiver) Eh? (replaces it)

(EFFECT 24. Knocking and shouting on all sides starts again. MUSIC 20. TWANKEY shoots to window and opens it, down to door D.L., and across to opening, where she disappears for a second then shoots on again to open door U.R., after which she has gathered such momentum that she continues round stage as PING, PONG, EMPRESS and EMPEROR enter, and chase after her TYPHOO enters U.R. dragging WISHEE at other end of lead. WISHEE still has the little shopping bag also some loose parcels.)

WISHEE: (to others) Excuse me. (MUSIC STOPS. All freeze. To TWANKEY) You did say two of flour.

TWANKEY: No, three.

WISHEE: Thank you.

(TYPHOO drags him off quickly D.R. MUSIC 21. The chase starts again until -)

PING:)
EMPEROR:) STOP!
EMPRESS:)
PONG:)

(MUSIC STOPS. TWANKEY stops suddenly in C.)

EMPRESS: Mrs Twankey, where is Aladdin?

TWANKEY: I don't know. You had him last. What did you do with him?

PONG: We lost him.

TWANKEY: Then you ought to be ashamed of yourselves. You're just a lot of careless nincompoops.

EMPRESS: Did you say -

PING: Nin -

PONG: Com -

EMPEROR: Poops?

TWANKEY: Yes, only quicker. Nincompoops.

PING:)   Mrs Twankey, do you dare to call the Pekin Police Force
PONG:)   nincompoops?

EMPRESS: And dost thou dare to call thy esteemed Empress a nincompoop?

TWANKEY: (dusting her with feather duster) Yes, I dost.

EMPRESS:)
PING:)   Oh.
PONG:)

EMPEROR: I'm quite sure you'd dare to call me a nincompoop, because after all, I am one.

EMPRESS: Oh shush! Search the house!

(PONG moves to grandfather clock. EMPEROR to cupboard. PING to oven. EMPRESS leans on R. of table. TYPHOO drags WISHEE on D.R. He has some more parcels. All freeze again.)

WISHEE: (to others) Excuse me. (to TWANKEY) Was it a dozen or half a dozen eggs?

TWANKEY: A dozen.

WISHEE: Thank you.

(TYPHOO drags him off D.L. All continue searching.)

PONG: There's something moving in here.

EMPRESS: (rushing U.R.) What is it?

PONG: The pendulum.

(As soon as EMPRESS has moved away from table, TWANKEY taps on it and it moves.)

EMPRESS: Tcha! (pushes PONG's head into clock)

(EMPRESS moves down to table's first position. TWANKEY taps on table and it stops. EMPRESS reacts suspiciously on not finding table where it was.)

EMPEROR: Do you know what's in this cupboard?

EMPRESS: (rushing U.L.) What?

EMPEROR: Nothing at all.

EMPRESS: Oh, tush!

(TWANKEY has knocked on table ,and it has moved further L. As EMPRESS moves down again she taps to stop it. EMPRESS again misses table.)

PING: Well, well, well.

EMPRESS: (rushing U.C.) What have you found?

PING: (takes baby's jacket from oven) A potato jacket.

EMPRESS: Tcha! (reacts on table again) Constable Pong, find out if there is anybody under that table.

PONG: Right. (lifting cloth slightly) Is there anybody there?

ALADDIN:)
ABANAZAR:)   No.

PONG: Thank you. There's nobody there.

EMPRESS: I'm sure there is. (to AUDIENCE) Will you tell me - is there anybody there?

(TWANKEY runs down to floats.)

TWANKEY: (to AUDIENCE) Say "No".

(AUDIENCE reaction)

EMPRESS: I didn't quite hear you. Tell me again. Is there anybody there?

(TWANKEY leads AUDIENCE in saying "No". The table moves remaining distance to opening D.L. and ALADDIN and ABANAZAR crawl out and run off.)

Then how did that table get there? It was over here a minute ago.

TWANKEY: It must have walked.

EMPRESS: How could it have walked?

TWANKEY: (crossing to L. of table to bring it back) Well, it's got legs, hasn't it?

EMPRESS: They were hiding under it and now they've escaped. Right, we'll have you for aiding and abetting.

TWANKEY: Oh no, you won't!

(MUSIC 22. As EMPRESS moves in towards her she buffets her in stomach with table and knocks her over. She lies gasping, as if winded. PONG moves in from L.)

(whipping cloth off table and throwing it over PONG) Nor you neither.

(PONG staggers around trying to get out of cloth. PING moves down to TWANKEY)

(plonking laundry basket over PING's head) And that goes for you too.

(TYPHOO drags WISHEE on from D.R. with even more parcels. MUSIC STOPS. All freeze.)

WISHEE: (to others) Excuse me. (to TWANKEY) One or two of
    pineapple chunks?

TWANKEY: Two.

WISHEE: Thank you.

(TYPHOO drags him off through window. MUSIC 23. EMPEROR starts to chase
TWANKEY, she thumbs nose at him, runs round table and up to cupboard,
where she opens door and steps to one side. EMPEROR runs into cupboard, she shuts door on him. PING has got out of basket and is helping
EMPRESS up. TWANKEY grabs picture from C., and - standing on chair
- crashes it over their heads; they try to move in opposite directions in
the frame. PING pulls the EMPRESS on to his back and TWANKEY
guides them off D.L. PONG has got the sheet off, TWANKEY grabs poker
from range, heats it for a second and turns to attack PONG. PONG uses
the sheet like a matador's cloak, TWANKEY holds the poker to her head
and crouches down, paws the ground and charges. PONG makes her pass
him to D.L. corner. He bows with his bottom towards her, just as she
turns. She touches him on bottom with poker and propels him through
D.L. door.

PONG: Ooohhh!!! Aaaaahhhhh!!!!!

(TWANKEY runs across to range, puts poker down and grabs breakable
plate from rack. She runs back to cupboard.)

TWANKEY: (opening cupboard door) Empie, you can come out now.

EMPEROR: (coming out, raising hat) Good afternoon, have you...

TWANKEY: (crowning him with plate) No.

(EMPEROR staggers about, TWANKEY guides him down L., then pushes
him off with her foot.

Victory! And he who laughs last - (moving away, she trips on rug, falls
and turns somersault) Drat that rug!

(BLACKOUT)

(Close traverse tabs)

MUSIC 24.

Scene Four - OUTSIDE THE LAUNDRY

(TABS. (Fly in frontcloth for Scene Five during scene.) MUSIC CONTINUES.
Enter EMPEROR L., staggering in a series of circles towards R., rubbing
his head. He is overtaken by PING and EMPRESS, still back to back in
picture frame, running from L. to R. All exit R. PONG enters L., clutching
his behind.)

PONG: Oo! Oo! Oo! (he runs off R. MUSIC STOPS, and he returns
immediately holding a block of ice to his behind) Ah! Ah! Ah! (he stops in
C.) That's better. But I don't know how I'll ever get over the shock of that
poker. Sugar - that's what I need for shock. Ah, bamboo cane sugar.
(he runs to the shoot.)

(AUDIENCE shout)

Aah! (he runs off L.)

(TYPHOO, with WISHEE dragging behind, bursts into auditorium. HOUSE
LIGHTS UP. WISHEE laden with even more parcels, paper carrier bags
etc.)

WISHEE: Yes, all right. We're here. (looks up onto stage) There's
nobody there. I think they must be having us on, don't you Typhoo?

(TYPHOO agrees and they move to catwalk. As they do PONG looks on L.,
sees them, drops to his knees and carefully crawls on stage, without ice,
around to bamboo. AUDIENCE shout.)

Yes, they're having a game with us - trying to make us think there's
somebody there now. What's that, there is? No, there isn't. There isn't,
is there, Typhoo?

(By this time they are on catwalk. HOUSE LIGHTS OUT. TYPHOO looks
across sees PONG, nods vigorously to WISHEE and points to PONG.)

(turns to look) There is! Oh, you naughty constable! You made me dis-
believe all these nice people. (to AUDIENCE) I'm so sorry.

(PONG is very shamefaced. TYPHOO admonishingly shakes her head at
him and beckons to him to come to her. He crosses to her. She motions
to him to turn round and bend down. He does so. She pulls her hand back
to give him a tremendous slap but WISHEE stops her and indicates to her
to be less violent. She moves her hand in a bit. He indicates to her to
move in a bit more. She does so reluctantly. He approves and she slaps
PONG gently.)

Let that be a lesson to you. What did you want my bamboo shoot for, anyway?

PONG: I just wanted a bit of sugar.

WISHEE: Sugar? I'll give you some sugar. I've got pounds of it here,
somewhere. There you are, take that. (gives PONG a large packet) And
that. (gives him another and pushes him off L.) Oh, and here's a bit more.
(throws a packet after him) That was silly of me. Now I'll have to go and
buy some more. Never mind, you take the rest of this stuff to Widow
Twankey while I'm buying the sugar. (he loads TYPHOO up with parcels)
There you are. Careful how you cross the road.

(TYPHOO nods and exits L.)

WISHEE: Now, shall I go to the Supermarket for it, or the little
     grocer's on the corner or to that new cut price store down the road? Well,
     the Supermarket's lump is a penny cheaper than the cut price's gran but
     the cut price's caster is twopence cheaper than the grocer's dem. On the
     other hand, the grocer gives Green Shield Stamps.

MUSIC 25.   "SHOPPING"

                         Shopping's most confusing in this cut-price age;
                              Doing all the shopping's not a joke.
                         If you go to help yourself
                         To the things along the shelf,
                              You'll find in twenty minutes that you're broke!
                         You merely want a cereal for breakfast,
                              And straight away your troubles have begun.
                         There's tuppence knocked off, then -
                         For an extra eight and ten
                              There's the very latest flick-knife for your son!

                         You've got the biscuits, tea and marge,
                         Some tinned cream small, and toothpaste large,
                         And cheese at sevenpence a bite,
                         And stuff that washes whiter white,
                         And special brands of stoneless fruits,
                         And special blacking for your boots,
                         And soaps and polishes galore
                         Prevent you walking through the door,
                         And just as you are going out,
                         Some paper we don't talk about;
                         Then tins of paste and jars of jam
                         And frozen peas and lumps of ham,
                         And more to eat and more to drink,
                         And stuff to clean the kitchen sink -
                         And once your little spree's begun
                         The final weight is half a ton!

                         You've made a little list of your requirements,
                         But the artful layout has you in its spell
                              And it gets you! You can't stop
                              Till you walk out of the shop
                         With a hundred thousand other things as well!
                         Shopping's most confusing in this cut-price age.
                         Your brow with perspiration is quite wet.
                              You stagger home with all the lot -
                              Then you find you haven't got
                         The thing you went out specially to get!

(BLACKOUT)

(Open traverse tabs)   MUSIC 26.

Scene Five - ON THE WAY TO THE CAVE

(Frontcloth, representing wild mountainous country. Movable piece in
R.C., of cloth for cave opening, with blasted tree and large marked rock
painted beside it. (If cloth is not used open tabs to reveal a 6ft flat with
the above details.) Enter ABANAZAR L., followed by a weary ALADDIN)

ALADDIN: (stopping L.C.) Oh uncle, can't we rest a little? I'm so
tired.

ABANAZAR: I care not a fig for thy tiredness. Come, onwards, boy.
We must waste no time.

ALADDIN: Well, we certainly haven't so far. We've been going all
day. Oh, uncle, I must stop for a while.

ABANAZAR: And I say we must go on, and - as I remember - your
mother bade you obey me in all things.

ALADDIN: I know, but you were nice then. The further we've gone the
nastier you've become. Anyway, I don't see how coming to this beastly
place will make me a rich man.

ABANAZAR: I have promised thee much gold - is that not enough?

ALADDIN: No, it isn't. I don't believe your promises any more. The
only gold I've seen so far is that ring on your finger. I know - give me
that to show you intend to keep your promise.

ABANAZAR: This ring? No! That you cannot have. 'Tis valuable to me.

ALADDIN: Then it would be valuable to me too.

ABANAZAR: Nay, 'tis a trumpery thing and of little worth.

ALADDIN: Well, it must be worth something or you wouldn't be so
keen to hang onto it, so I'm not going to move till you give it to me.

ABANAZAR: Tcha! Take the ring then! (wrenches ring from finger and
gives it to ALADDIN) Curse the boy. Now let us proceed.

(They move R., ALADDIN examining the ring.)

Ah! This is it, if I mistake not. Aye, here the withered tree, and here
the rock with the mark upon it. Stand back, Aladdin, and I will show thee
wonders.

(ABANAZAR faces the backcloth and makes magic passes with hands.
Lights dim. MUSIC 27.)

Ye spirit guardians of these rocks,
'Tis time to loose thy magic locks.
In name of Suleyman I call
Break ope this solid seeming wall -
Come lightning! Come crash of thunder!
Cause the rocks to burst asunder!

(Lights flicker, lightning flash and EFFECT 25 thunder crack. White flash
then EFFECT 26 heavy rumbling sound as the cave opens. ALADDIN has
run L. frightened.)

ABANAZAR: There, 'tis done. Come boy, do not be afeared. Look within the cave. What seest thou?

ALADDIN: (very fearfully looking into cave) Oh, uncle it's full of gold and silver and jewels.

ABANAZAR: Did I not promise thee great wealth? And 'tis all thine. You may take as much as you desire - but after you have done what I wish. Now listen well - somewhere in the cave lies hid a lamp.

ALADDIN: A lamp?

ABANAZAR: Aye, 'tis a foolish whim of mine to have it. First, procure this lamp and hand it up to me, and then load thyself with riches. You understand me, boy? First the lamp.

ALADDIN: Yes, all right, uncle.

ABANAZAR: Go then.

ALADDIN: (steps into cave) I'm in, uncle.

ABANAZAR: Good, good.

ALADDIN: (jumps out) I'm out again.

ABANAZAR: (threateningly) Boy - !

ALADDIN: (jumps in) I'm in again.

ABANAZAR: Ah.

ALADDIN: I'm out. (jumps out)

(ABANAZAR threatens)

(jumps in) I'm in. (jumps out) I'm out.

ABANAZAR: Cease this pestilential hopscotch!

ALADDIN: But, uncle, I'm frightened.

ABANAZAR: Put thy fears at rest. Naught shall harm thee while I am here. Quickly, go!

ALADDIN: All right. (gets into cave) I'm going, uncle.

ABANAZAR: Yes, yes.

(ALADDIN disappears to R.)

Aha!

ALADDIN: (poking his head out) I've gone. (withdraws head)

(Close traverse tabs. Fly-out cloth.)

ABANAZAR: So, now the magic lamp is almost mine! And once I have it safely in my hands, I'll seal the cave and leave Aladdin here - to die! (laughs fiendishly)

(EFFECT 27 Thunder rolls and lightning. MUSIC 28.)

(BLACKOUT - open traverse tabs)

Scene Six - THE MAGIC CAVE OF JEWELS

(Full set. Gauze cloth behind rostrum painted to represent cave wall.
Cut-out piece set obliquely on R. of rostrum to represent cave opening.
(If a gauze is not possible, have gauze-filled frame cut-outs, representing rocks set on back of rostrum and mounted on battens running off
stage by which they can slowly be pulled off at end of scene.) Steps on
rostrum leading down from cave opening masked by cut-out rock piece
on front of rostrum. Steps leading down from C. of rostrum to stage.
Rock wing R. Rock wing L. Magic lamp on pedestal L.C. by steps.
Gold and jewel effects heaped about wherever possible. ALADDIN
discovered halfway down steps from opening.)

ALADDIN: (moving down) Oh, uncle, it's wonderful! I've never seen
so many beautiful things - but it's a bit eerie too. I say, uncle, just come
and look at some of these diamonds - they're the size of your fist - and
oh! What lovely emeralds. (reaches rostrum)

ABANAZAR: (poking head through opening) Ay, but never mind the
jewels, my boy. Have you found the lamp?

ALADDIN: Not yet, uncle. (moving slowly down steps from rostrum
to stage) There's such a lot of wonderful things to look at. Great nuggets
of gold and bars of silver. And look - here's ivory too.

ABANAZAR: The lamp, Aladdin, find the lamp!

ALADDIN: Ooh, it is creepy down here. I don't think I'll go any
further.

ABANAZAR: You must! You must!

ALADDIN: It's all very well to say "you must", but you're not where
I am.

ABANAZAR: Have I not told thee there is naught to fear?

ALADDIN: (going down a little further) Well, I can't see a lamp anywhere. I don't think it's here.

ABANAZAR: What? It must be!

ALADDIN: How do you know? Wait. I think I can see it.

ABANAZAR: Ah!

ALADDIN: (at pedestal) Yes, here it is, uncle.

ABANAZAR: Good, then quickly let me have it.

ALADDIN: (slowly mounting steps with lamp) It's a very nasty dirty
old lamp. What do you want it for?

ABANAZAR: That matters not. Come give it me, and hurry.

ALADDIN: Why are you so anxious to have it?

ABANAZAR: No, no, not anxious, my boy. But - but it is cold here and
I would have done as soon as possible. So let me have the lamp and then
go choose thy riches.

ALADDIN: But what's the use of it?

ABANAZAR: Will thy idle questions never cease? Give me the lamp!

ALADDIN: Oh, all right, here you are.

ABANAZAR: (stretching his hands out eagerly) Ah!

ALADDIN: No, if you want it so much, come and get it yourself.

ABANAZAR: Ten thousand maledictions. Your taunts exhaust my
patience! I grant you but one last chance, Aladdin. Will you, or will you
not give me the lamp?

ALADDIN: No.

ABANAZAR: Then hear my curse and perish! -
MUSIC 29.
Thou dolt, thou dunderhead baboon!
Thou addlepated lackwit loon,
Ne'er again shalt thou roam free
The sunlight or the stars to see
But here remain till crack of doom
This cave thy prison - and thy tomb!
Come, spirit guardians of the rocks,
Make fast again thy magic locks.
In name of Suleyman I say,
Shut out once more all light of day,
Come elemental furies - rave!
Exert thy might - seal up the cave!

(Lightning and **EFFECT 28 thunder crash**. White flash and **EFFECT 29**
heavy rumbling sound as cave door begins to close to the accompaniment
of ABANAZAR's fiendish laughter. ALADDIN runs up the steps.)

ALADDIN: No, uncle, wait! Wait! Don't leave me here!

(Cave door is not quite to, ALADDIN vainly endeavours to stop it.)

Uncle! Uncle! It's closing! I can't stop it. I can't stop it!

(Door closes, ALADDIN still tries to pull it back.)

Uncle, open the cave! Open the cave! Let me out! I'll let you have the
lamp. I'll let you have anything, only let me out! (slight pause) Uncle,
open the cave! Open the cave! (pause) Uncle, come back! (pause) No
good. Oh, why didn't I let him have the lamp? Why should I worry why
he wanted it? There might be lots of reasons. Perhaps it's solid gold
underneath all this dirt. (is about to clean it with sleeve, but stops) But
no - there's plenty more gold here, if that's what he wanted. Anyway,
what does it matter? Because I wouldn't let him have it I'm imprisoned
here forever. For ever? No, no. There must be some other way out.
(runs U.R.) Here? No, solid rock. (runs D.R.) Then here? (runs L.)
Over here? (runs U.L.) Or here? No. (returns wearily to C. and sits
on bottom step) Oh dear - no, I must try to keep cheerful; and it is rather
funny really. Here I am, surrounded by riches, and I'm going to starve
to death! No, maybe it's not so funny after all. Keeping cheerful isn't
so easy when you're all alone in a cold and damp and gloomy cave like

ALADDIN: (continued) this. Well, I might be able to make it a bit
less gloomy if I could light this lamp. I wonder if it's got a wick in it?
It's so covered with dirt I can't really tell.

(Rubs lamp with sleeve. Cymbal roll and crash, blue flash. MUSIC 30.
SLAVE OF LAMP leaps on from R. ALADDIN jumps away, scared.
SLAVE salaams.)

S. OF LAMP: My master calls and I am here.

ALADDIN: Cripes! I say, how did you appear?

S. OF LAMP: Whoever holds the lamp I serve
In ev'rything without reserve.
You rubb'd the lamp and summon'd me.

ALADDIN: But who you are I still don't see.

S. OF LAMP: Slave of the magic lamp am I.
But state thy wish and I'll comply.

ALADDIN: A magic lamp! Ah, now I know
Why Abanazar wish'd it so.
But can you do anything I ask?

S. OF LAMP: However small or large the task
I can perform it. What would you?
A fountain run with mountain dew?
A bathing lake of asses' milk,
And rarer wonders of that ilk?
A palace, wealth beyond compare,
Beauteous maids? - Aught of earth and air.

ALADDIN: Well, if it wouldn't seem too rude,
I'm dying for a bite of food.

S. OF LAMP: Master, rare dishes and choice meat
Shall be prepar'd for thee to eat.

ALADDIN: No, no. A snack is all I need.

S. OF LAMP: Then 'tis a very simple deed. (MUSIC 31. Produces
plate of sandwiches.)

ALADDIN: Oh - thanks.

S. OF LAMP: What more dost thou require?

ALADDIN: To leave this cave's my chief desire.

S. OF LAMP: Another simple deed, my lord,
Most swiftly done, so rest assur'd.
But first, I prithee, come with me
That thou may richly clothed be.

ALADDIN: Well, this suit has seen better days.

S. OF LAMP: Then come, on silks and satins gaze,
O'er cloth of gold and velvets muse,
And from them princely raiment choose;
And while you thus your form enhance

S. OF LAMP: (continued)
                        To entertain thee with their dance
                        The guardians of this cave I'll call
                        From where they hide in niche of wall.

(S. OF LAMP hands ALADDIN off R.)

                        Come spirits!

MUSIC 32.

(BALLET, led by SLAVE OF LAMP. Toward end of ballet ALADDIN is
led on by CHORUS. He is magnificently attired.)

                        Now, master thou shalt homeward go;
                        To free thee, I'll my power show. (MUSIC 33.)
                        All the ground shall shake and rumble
                        And the wall to powder crumble.

(SLAVE OF LAMP takes up attitude facing back, and makes magic passes.
EFFECT 30. Thunder rolls. Lightning flashes. Lights up behind gauze to
reveal evening sky effect on cyclorama. SLAVE makes another pass.
EFFECT 31. More thunder and lightning and gauze cloth is taken up. Dawn
begins to break on the skycloth as ALADDIN mounts steps, holding lamp
and takes up triumphant position on rostrum.)

(CURTAIN.)

(CURTAIN up for tableau.)

(CURTAIN.)

MUSIC 34 ENTR'ACTE

PART TWO

Scene Seven - WIDOW TWANKEY's
LAUNDERETTE

(The set is as in Scene Three, but now about half way U.S., and a little
to L. of C. is a wooden frame unit representing five washing machines,
which are numbered from 1 to 5 from the R. (1 to 4 are about 1ft. 9in.
wide, No. 5 is a narrow one only about 1ft wide) Each has a practical
door with a round porthole in it which we can see through, and each has a
practical trap door on top (larger than reality) for putting soap in. The
depth of the unit should be about 2ft. and there should be a black drape
at the back to conceal the three people necessary to work the doors. This
they do by means of canes attached to the C. top of the doors and extend-
ing through the black drape, which they push to open doors and pull to
shut. Two people work two machines each and the third one. Along the
top and at the back, should be an upraised panel with the setting control
knobs for each machine. On the front R. hand side of each machine is a
red light. Set inside Nos. 2 to 5 are cardboard replicas of certain
garments. In front of the machines is a bench big enough to seat 5. Set
behind the unit is a large prop gluepot marked GLUE. To the R. of the
unit set obliquely is the kitchen table with a set of scales on upstage end
and a prop till on downstage. There is also a telephone, a large packet
marked WIFF, and ten soap cups on two trays of five each on table.
Under the table is a laundry basket with a soda syphon in it and seven
washboards. Above the U.S. end of the table is a large mangle. In front
of D.R. entrance is a large prop iron. Below the window is a large round
unit labelled SPIN DRYER, which has a practical lid but no base.)

(The CHORUS are discovered sitting on bench singing opening number,
during which they put washing from the launderette type bags they carry
into the machines, add powder, take the washing out, put it in the spin
dryer and finally return it to their bags.)

MUSIC 35.   "WIDOW TWANKEY'S LAUNDERETTE"

CHORUS: At Widow Twankey's Launderette
                            Into machines we're squashing
                            A lot of dirty washing
                                 As easy as can be.
                            It's better than a washing tub,
                            For here you do not have to scrub,
                            Round and around and around they whirl,
                            Getting our things in a terrible twirl,
                                 Sing hey for washing day!

                            At Widow Twankey's Launderette
                            We like a little prattling,
                            A bit of tittle-tattling
                                 To pass the time away.
                            It's better than a garden wall
                            For here you do not risk a fall.
                            Cackle and waggle our tongues do go

CHORUS: (continued)
Spreading our gossip for all to know,
Sing hey for washing day!

At Widow Twankey's Launderette,
Though we'd go on for ever
We have our talk to sever
When our machines all stop.
We take our things out then we fly
To spin them round and get them dry.
This is the easier modern way,
Which leaves us plenty of time to say
Sing hey for washing day!

CHORUS GIRL: Ooh, doesn't work make you hungry?

ANOTHER: Well, there's a bamboo shoot here.

ALL. Let's take it.

(They move to do so. AUDIENCE shout and WISHEE pops up from behind the washing machines.)

WISHEE: Did someone call? Ah, yes, thank you. (coming round L. end of machines) Now, now, ladies.

CHORUS: (backing away from shoot) Oh, what a pity.

(WIDOW TWANKEY enters D.R.)

TWANKEY: Ah, good morning, good morning, good morning. (she trips and falls over iron) Who left that there? (rising and putting iron on range and then moving to behind table) Well, I'm sure you all enjoyed a really good wash for a change.

CHORUS: We beg your pardon?

TWANKEY: I mean in my new machines. I hope you all had a good two and ninepence worth?

CHORUS: No.

TWANKEY:)
WISHEE:) No?

CHORUS: No. As there was no one here we didn't pay anything. Good morning. (they exit D.L.)

TWANKEY: Well, of all the cheek. Next time they call I'll put in my special clothes rippers and buttons whippers.

(EFFECT 32. Telephone bell rings. TWANKEY lifts receiver on table.)

(into phone) Widow Twankey's Launderette at your service.

FEMALE VOICE: (off, miked if possible) Mrs Slo Lee here. I'm sending you some laundry for servicing in your launderette.

TWANKEY: Oh yes, Mrs Slo Lee. How are you sending it, Mrs Slo Lee?

VOICE: Quick-lee.

(A bundle flies through the window hitting WISHEE and knocking him over. He rises rubbing his head.)

WISHEE: I say, really.

TWANKEY: Never mind, dear. We'll charge her an extra tanner for wear and tear. Pop it in Number One.

(WISHEE does so and slams door shut. All the others open. He looks a little puzzled, shuts No. 2 tentatively, then 3, 4 and 5 with increasing confidence. As soon as he shuts No. 5, No. 1 springs open. He hurries to it, shuts it gently, is satisfied, shrugs and moves away happily to L. The whole lot open.

(moving round to machines) I don't think you've quite got the knack, dear. Look, like this. Stand clear of the doors, please. (She moves along from 1 to 5, shutting them like a train porter and blowing a whistle at the end of the line) You see. That's known as the (local allusion) technique. It never fails.

(No. 1 shoots open. Enraged she runs to shut it. It shuts itself, nipping her fingers.)

Ow! It's vicious. (setting dial on No. 1) Anyway, now we can start Mrs Slo Lee off. (moves behind table to put some soap powder in a cup)

(The red light comes up on No. 1)

WISHEE: Ready for first soaping.

(He takes cup and puts powder in. He replaces cup. TWANKEY refills it. The red light comes up again.)

Ready for second soaping.

(WISHEE puts soap in. The red light goes out. WISHEE replaces cup.)

Ready for spin dryer.

TWANKEY: Marvellously quick these new machines.

WISHEE: (opens door of No. 1) I can't find it. It's disappeared. Clean disappeared.

TWANKEY: Really? Oh well, so long as it's clean that's something. I'll send her a note saying "All wash lost in wash...better luck next time." Well, now we need some more customers.

(Enter EMPRESS, PING and PONG with laundry bags. WISHEE moves behind table, U.S. end.)

ALL: Good morning. We've come to do our washing.

TWANKEY:)
WISHEE:)   How wise.

(Enter EMPEROR with laundry bag.)

EMPEROR: Good morning. I've come to -

TWANKEY:)
WISHEE:)   - do your washing?

EMPEROR: No, my coms.

TWANKEY:)
WISHEE:)   How revolutionary!

WISHEE: Well, by a stroke of luck you've come to just the right place. This is a launderette.

EMPEROR:)
PING:)
PONG:)   How -
EMPRESS:)

TWANKEY:)
WISHEE:)   Yes?

OTHERS: Do you do.

(All shake hands.)

TWANKEY: Now, we only need one more customer and we've got a full house.

(TYPHOO runs in and points eagerly to herself.)

Typhoo. But you haven't got any clothes to wash.

(TYPHOO nods and holds up her collar.)

Yes, of course, your collar. Well, join the queue. Empress will you put your washing on the scales, please?

(EMPRESS does so. WISHEE looks at the weight registered.)

WISHEE: Over-weight.

EMPRESS: But it can't be. I've only brought a nightie and a hanky.

TWANKEY: Is it an embroidered hanky?

EMPRESS: Only with my initial.

TWANKEY: Ah, that explains it. Initials weigh very heavy. Three-pence extra for overweight. Three shillings, please.

(The EMPRESS indignantly gives her money.)

Thank you. (puts money in till drawer, shuts drawer and it comes through other side hitting EMPRESS.)

EMPRESS: Look out, woman!

TWANKEY: Sorry. Number four, please.

EMPRESS: Very well. (goes to No. 4)

WISHEE: (to PING) On the scales, please.

(PING puts laundry bag on scales)

WISHEE: (continued) Overweight.

PING: But I've only got one vest and a shirt.

TWANKEY: Has the shirt got buttonholes in it?

PING: Of course.

TWANKEY: There you are, then - all that space. Ever so heavy.
    Three shillings, please.

    (PING reluctantly gives money)

    Thank you. (opens drawer, puts money in. Shuts drawer and buffets
    PING.)

PING: Ooh!

TWANKEY: Sorry. Number three, please.

    (PING moves to No. 3)

WISHEE: (to PONG) On the scales, please.

PONG: Right. (starts to climb on scales)

WISHEE: No, not you, the washing.

PONG: Oh, sorry.

WISHEE: Overweight.

PONG: But I've only got a pair of pants.

TWANKEY: Well, there you are - pants - all that heavy breathing.
    Three shillings, please.

    (PONG gives her money)

    Thank you. (opens drawer, puts money in)

    Oh, mind out.

PONG: What for?

TWANKEY: This. (shuts drawer and hits PONG)

PONG: Ah, thanks for telling me.

TWANKEY: Number two please.

    (PONG moves to No. 2)

WISHEE: (to EMPEROR) On the scales, please.

    (EMPEROR puts washing on scales)

    Overweight.

EMPEROR: Well, just a little, but I'm on a diet.

WISHEE: I mean your laundry's overweight.

EMPEROR: Is it? Well, I'll put that on a diet too. Two and nine, I
    believe. (hands TWANKEY money) Thank you.

TWANKEY: (shrugs) Thank you.

(Opens drawer puts money in. EMPEROR drops bag and bends to pick it up just as she is shutting drawer and she misses him.)

That's funny I missed.

EMPEROR: (straightens up) Missed what? (pushes drawer through from his side and hits her)

TWANKEY: That. Number one please.

(EMPEROR moves to No. 1)

WISHEE: (to TYPHOO) On the scales, please.

(TYPHOO puts collar on scales.)

Underweight.

TWANKEY: Really? Well, you'd better have one on the house then. You can have the machine we keep for tall thin people. Number five.

(TYPHOO moves to No. 5. They proceed to take stuff out of bags. WISHEE puts scales under table.)

EMPEROR: (proudly holding up a pair of coms with large crest on seat) These are my coms.

TWANKEY: Oh, how ducky.

WISHEE: (pointing to crest) Don't you find that a bit uncomfortable?

EMPEROR: Yes, but it makes a big impression. (puts them in machine)

PONG: (proudly holding up a rather holey pair of pants) These are my pants.

WISHEE: But they're full of holes.

PONG: Of course they are. I couldn't get into 'em if they weren't. (puts them in his machine)

PING: (proudly holding up shirt) This is my shirt.

PONG: Are you sure? It looks like mine.

PING: Well, it isn't.

PONG: (grabbing hold of it) It is.

PING: (pulling one way) It isn't.

PONG: (pulling other way) It is.

(It tears in half. (poppered join))

(looks at his half) Oh, sorry it is yours. (gives it back to PONG)

TWANKEY: Never mind. Get the glue and pour a little in Ping's machine, Wishee.

(EMPRESS and TYPHOO have put their laundry in)

WISHEE: Righto. (he moves to behind machines, pours some glue from gluepot into PING's machine and sets the 5 dials and disappears behind unit)

EMPRESS: Don't we get some soap powder?

TWANKEY: Yes just as soon as the red light comes on.

EMPRESS: What soap powder is it?

TWANKEY: Well, we always use -

(WISHEE's face appears in the porthole of No. 3)

WISHEE: Stadirt! (holds up card in front of his face with the name on) Ladies, are you tired of having to put on (pulls down card to reveal himself in dark glasses) dark glasses every time you look at your washing. Then use Stadirt, the only soap powder with the magic ingredient Blakanbluinite. (holds up card with name on) Blakanbluinite literally pummels your clothes into greyness. (takes card down) So remember only with Stadirt can you get that dulling, dulling, dulling grey. (holds up Stadirt card) Stadirt.

TWANKEY: Well I never. Twiddle the knob and see if you can get the BBC.

(PING twiddles knob and the card and WISHEE disappear. The red lights come up.)

Oh pity. Actually we don't use that. We always use some Wiff. (holds up packet and fills soap cups with one movement)

PING: Some Wiff? Some Wiff what?

TWANKEY: Not wiff anything. (moves round with the cups on a little tray)

PONG: Oh, wiffout.

TWANKEY: (chucking a cup in No. 1) No Wiffin! And here's some for the rest of you.

(They take cups and pour them into their machines. The red lights go out)

OTHERS: What do we do now?

WISHEE: (appearing from behind machines) Watch for the second red light, then you get another whiff of Wiff.   (moves to behind table)

MUSIC 36.

(The five sit on the bench backs to audience staring at their machines. Gradually their heads start to go round in time together, getting quicker and quicker until suddenly the red lights go on again and they jump up.)

THE FOUR: More Wiff!

TWANKEY: Wait a jiff!

(She swiftly pours them out as before. WISHEE rushes out with the cupfuls and hands them round and they put them in. WISHEE returns to behind table. MUSIC 37. The five sit looking at their machines, their heads going

(round faster and faster then slowing down and stopping and each head flops in slumber on his neighbour's R. shoulder excepting, of course, the EMPEROR's. All snore. He gradually leans further and further to his L. and topples off the end of bench so that the remainder fall down and all wake up.)

TWANKEY: (continued) Right. All out! (doors fly open)

(TYPHOO takes out her collar. It is completely stiff, tries to bend it but can't and holds it out enquiringly.)

WISHEE: (taking it) Well, that's funny. Never mind, Typhoo. It's a stiff collar now.

EMPRESS: But all my washing's stiff too. (holds out cardboard replica of nightie)

PING: And mine. (holds out cardboard replica of vest)

PONG: And mine. (holds out cardboard replica of a sock)

WISHEE: (to EMPEROR) What about yours?

EMPEROR: I can't find mine at all.

WISHEE: Really? We've had that trouble with number one before.

PING:)
PONG:)   But how did this happen?
EMPRESS:)

TWANKEY: Well, perhaps - er (looks at Wiff packet) Hm. Well what do you know - this Wiff isn't soap powder at all. It's starch. How very funny. (throws packet off, laughs then stops) Oh well, it'll save on the ironing, won't it? Anyway you can still have a go in the spin dryer.

(WISHEE collects replicas from EMPRESS and PING and moves to spin dryer.)

PONG: But mine doesn't need drying. It's too dry already.

TWANKEY: Oh, I can soon deal with that for you. (brings up soda syphon and squirts it at PONG not getting much on his laundry) Ooh dear, my aim's not very good, is it? Never mind, find a hanger and drip dry yourself.

(EMPEROR, still searching for his coms, falls into his machine and the door shuts on him.)

EMPEROR: Help! Help!

TWANKEY: Oh I say, just look what's happened now.

(We see the EMPEROR's face going round and round in the porthole. The EMPEROR's head pops up through the trap door at the top.)

EMPEROR: I'm getting giddy. (disappears and rotates again)

EMPRESS: Don't all just stand there - do something.

TWANKEY: I am. I'm waiting for the red light to come up to give him

TWANKEY: (continued) his first soaping.

EMPRESS: Nonsense, get him out!

(TWANKEY, PING and PONG open door and extricate EMPEROR.)

TWANKEY: Ooh, I'm afraid he's rather wet. We'd better put him in
the spin dryer.

(They lift him and carry him over to spin dryer and dump him in, helped
by WISHEE.)

TWANKEY: There, soon have him all right. (lifts lid) Are you all
right, Empie? (shuts lid) Oh yes, he's rotating lovely.

EMPRESS: But is he dry yet? He'll catch his death.

TWANKEY: (lifts lid again) Ooh, I can't find him.

WISHEE: He must have shrunk.

EMPRESS: Oh really, this is very careless of you, Mrs Twankey.

(PING and PONG lift the whole spin dryer up so that the EMPEROR is left
on floor. PING looks through one end and PONG the other. Others look
towards them expectantly.)

PING: Can you see anything?

PONG: Yes.

PING: What?

PONG: You.

(TYPHOO tugs at WISHEE's sleeve and points to EMPEROR.)

WISHEE: Oh, here he .s.

EMPRESS: Is he dry yet?

WISHEE: (touching him to see) Not quite.

TWANKEY: Let's wring him out then. I expect he'll go through the
mangle.

(TWANKEY, WISHEE, PING and PONG carry EMPEROR to mangle.
EMPRESS clears the cash register and telephone off the table. TWANKEY
turns handle and they start to push him face down with arms outstretched
through the mangle but get stuck by his head. They try again with the
same result. The third time the EMPEROR goes smoothly through.)

Now turn him over and let's give him a bit of an iron.

(They turn him over onto his back but his head dangles down over D. S.
end of table. His feet rest on topmost roller of mangle.)

Have to pull him up a bit.

(She turns mangle handle and EMPEROR slides forward on table.)

Bring us the iron.

PING: (goes to it from range) Is it hot? (licks his finger to test it)

PING: (continued)   Ow, yes! (shakes finger vigorously)

(TWANKEY plonks the iron down on EMPEROR's stomach which makes him wriggle. She irons up to his face and goes delicately round his nose.)

TWANKEY: (sings) I don't want to set the Emperor on fire. (she irons down him and does the soles of his feet, which seem to tickle him. She then plonks the iron back on his stomach and leaves it.) There now he's as dry as a bone.

EMPEROR: Ow!

TWANKEY: Sorry.

(TWANKEY takes iron off and hands it to PONG who takes it by the base and drops it on PING's feet.)

PING:)
PONG:)   Ooowww!

TWANKEY: Silly boys.

EMPRESS: Are you all right now, Emperor?

EMPEROR: (rising from table) Yes, of course, my dear, why shouldn't I be? But I don't think I like this new fangled washing.

TWANKEY: Well, to tell you the truth, neither do I. (getting washboards) Give me the old fashioned wash on the washboard.

(Each takes a washboard. (All will need to carry thimbles which they now put on and play with on the washboards as they sing.))

MUSIC 38. "WASHBOARD BLUES"

ALL: You take a large pile of laundry,
                  And you dump it in the water,

TWANKEY: And then you soap, soap, soap till the suds are solid
                  That's the way to get clean!

PING, PONG,
WISHEE, EMP: You take a large pile, etc.
& EMPRESS
PING: And then you rub, rub, rub till the water's filthy

TWANKEY: Soap, soap, soap, etc.

BOTH: That's the way to get clean!

PONG, WISHEE
EMP & EMPRESS: You take a large pile, etc.,

PONG: And then you bash, bash, bash with a wooden ladle -

PING: Rub, rub, rub, etc.,

TWANKEY: Soap, soap, soap, etc.

ALL 3:   That's the way to get clean!

WISHEE, EMP
& EMPRESS: You take a large pile, etc.

WISHEE:	And then you rinse, rinse, rinse till you've no more water -
PONG:	Bash, bash, bash, etc.,
PING:	Rub, rub, rub, etc.,
TWANKEY:	Soap, soap, soap, etc.
ALL 4:	That's the way to get clean!
EMP & EMPRESS:	You take a large pile, etc.,
EMPEROR:	And then you hang, hang, hang on a nice dry morning -
WISHEE:	Rinse, rinse, rinse, etc.,
PONG:	Bash, bash, bash, etc.,
PING:	Rub, rub, rub, etc.,
TWANKEY:	Soap, soap, soap, etc.
ALL 5:	That's the way to get clean!
EMPRESS:	You take a large pile, etc., And then you iron, iron, iron in a nice warm kitchen -
EMPEROR:	Hang, hang, hang, etc.,
WISHEE:	Rinse, rinse, rinse, etc.,
PONG:	Bash, bash, bash, etc.,
PING:	Rub, rub, rub, etc.,
TWANKEY:	Soap, soap, soap, etc.
ALL:	That's the way to get clean!

(All exit except TWANKEY.)

TWANKEY: Well, I suppose I'd better clear up in case any more customers drop in. (picks up iron from where PONG dropped it)

ALADDIN: (off L.) Mother! Mother!

TWANKEY: Aladdin!

(ALADDIN enters D. L.)

My boy! My boy! (moving round him admiringly) Oh I say, what a lovely gents natty you've got on.

ALADDIN: Mother, we're rich - rich as anything! (producing some large diamonds) Look!

TWANKEY: (taking one) Hm, diamonds. DIAMONDS! (drops iron on foot) O'W! (holds foot out to ALADDIN) Kiss it better, dear.

(He blows it a kiss. She puts iron on range.)

Thank you dear. Well, I must say your uncle Abey has certainly done you proud.

ALADDIN: Abanazar? Oh no, he hasn't. In fact, he tried to kill me.

TWANKEY: He didn't!

ALADDIN: He did. He sealed me up in a cave and left me there to die.

TWANKEY: Oh, the old - asterisk! But in that case who did give you all these precious jewels?

ALADDIN: Ah-ha!

TWANKEY: And what did you bring that dirty old lamp home for?

ALADDIN: Because it's the most precious thing of all.

TWANKEY: It doesn't look very precious to me - rather a nasty looking object. Here, let me clean it up a bit.

ALADDIN: No, mother, wait -

(Too late, she has taken lamp, which hangs by ALADDIN's waist and is rubbing it with her apron. Cymbal roll and crash. Blue flash, BLACK-OUT. MUSIC 39. SLAVE OF LAMP jumps on from R. TWANKEY screams and falls down. LIGHTS UP)

S. OF LAMP: My master calls and I am here.

TWANKEY: Ow, help me up, I've gone all queer!

(ALADDIN crosses and helps her up.)

                    My boy, I think - if you don't mind -
                    I'll better feel when I've reclined.

ALADDIN: Don't go, mother, it's just the djinn.

TWANKEY: I thought as much. Don't rub it in. (exits D.R.)

ALADDIN: I fear it was a false alarm
                    That call'd you. Still, it's done no harm
                    For there is something I would ask.

S. OF LAMP: My lord, inform me of the task.

ALADDIN: Can you a palace build for me?

S. OF LAMP: At once, O master. It shall be
                    From countless grains of stardust built;
                    The walls - with sunbeams richly gilt -
                    Towering high into the sky
                    Neath roof of lapis lazuli.
                    And now, what can I grant thee more?

ALADDIN: Only to see Baldroubadour.

(SLAVE OF LAMP salaams, makes magic pass. Blue flash, cymbal crash, BLACKOUT, in which SLAVE exits and PRINCESS BALDROUBA-DOUR enters. EFFECT 33. Wind noise. LIGHTS UP.)

PRINCESS B: Aladdin! Aladdin, this isn't a dream, is it?

ALADDIN: I don't think so.

PRINCESS B: Oh, I'm so glad. You see, I came here so quickly I
    thought it must be. Oh, Aladdin, you've been away so long.

ALADDIN: Well, only a day or so.

PRINCESS B: Oh, no, I'm sure it was a century or so. And I must have
    aged terribly. But you will still marry me, won't you?

ALADDIN: Of course I will. I was just going to ask you.

PRINCESS B: Too late - I thought of it first. Aladdin, will you marry
    me?

ALADDIN: Well, provided that your father -

PRINCESS B: As your princess I order you to say "yes" immediately.

ALADDIN: Yes - immediately.

PRINCESS B: That's all right then. And if we're to be married
    immediately, we'd better make it Wednesday.

ALADDIN: Wednesday - but that's the day after tomorrow.

PRINCESS B: Then let's make it tomorrow. I don't believe in long
    engagements.

ALADDIN: But what about your father and mother?

PRINCESS B: Oh, as long as you can offer them plenty of money you'll
    be all right.

ALADDIN: That's easy. I'll go and see them at once.

PRINCESS B: Well, not quite at once. First you can tell me that you
    love me.

ALADDIN: Don't you know I do?

PRINCESS B: Of course, but I like to hear you saying it.

MUSIC 40.   (Reprise: "HAS ANYBODY SEEN MY HEART".)

    (BLACKOUT.)

MUSIC 41.   (Close traverse tabs fly in frontcloth for Scene Eight if used.)

Scene Eight - THE EMPEROR'S AUDIENCE
CHAMBER

(Frontcloth or tabs. If cloth is used open tabs as soon as convenient
during scene. Enter PING and PONG R., carrying a double throne chair.
They circle round to music and place it at an angle R.C. then stand in C.,
PING L., PONG R.)

PING & PONG: Their illustrious Majesties the Emperor and Empress!

MUSIC 42.
(Fanfare. Enter EMPEROR and EMPRESS R., EMPEROR U.S. They stop
in front of throne chair. PING and PONG bow to them. They bow to PING
and PONG and then turn inwards to bow to each other and bump heads.)

EMPRESS: Emperor, do be more careful.

EMPEROR: Sorry, my dear.

(They sit.)

EMPRESS: Now I think you're ready, Emperor?

EMPEROR: Am I, my dear? What for?

EMPRESS: To give audience, of course. Today's your audience
giving day.

(Enter ALADDIN L.)

Who is this?

ALADDIN: I'm Ala -

EMPRESS: Don't tell us. Tell them.

ALADDIN: Sorry. (to PONG) I'm Aladdin.

PONG: (to PING) He's Aladdin.

PING: (to EMPEROR) He's Aladdin.

EMPEROR: (to EMPRESS) He's Aladdin.

EMPRESS: Aladdin what?

EMPEROR: Oh, you've met him before, have you? How do you do, Mr
What?

ALADDIN: But Sire, my name is not What.

EMPEROR: Oh, Aladdin Notwhat. He's a different Aladdin to the one
you know, dear.

EMPRESS: I don't know any Aladdins. Though wait a minute, the name
has a familiar ring to it. What does he want?

EMPEROR: Ah there you have me. What do you want, Mr - er - em - ?

ALADDIN: Sire, I -

EMPEROR: No, no, don't tell me. I'll get it in a minute - Mr - er -
it's on the tip of my -

ALADDIN: Sire - What I -

EMPEROR: That's it! What! I told you I'd get it. I never forget a
    name, you know.

EMPRESS: But his name is not What.

EMPEROR: So it is.

EMPRESS: What is?

EMPEROR: No, Notwhat is. I thought you said you knew him?

EMPRESS: I do not know him. And furthermore I don't want to know
    him, but I do want to know what he is doing here.

EMPEROR: And so you shall, my dear. Now, what are you doing here,
    Whatnot?

ALADDIN: Sire, I come to ask for your daughter's hand in marriage.

EMPRESS: You WHAT!

EMPEROR: No, Notwhat.

EMPRESS: Ah, now I remember him, Emperor. He's the scoundrel
    we caught with our daughter before.

EMPEROR: There, I knew we'd met. Oh yes, an excellent chap.

EMPRESS: Are you out of your Chinese mind, Emperor? Have him
    beheaded twice.

ALADDIN: Sire, hear me out. I did not come empty handed. (pro-
    ducing jewels) See.

EMPRESS: Have him beheaded once.

EMPEROR: They're whoppers.

EMPRESS: (to EMPEROR) Ssh! (to ALADDIN) Very poor specimens.
    Have you any more?

ALADDIN: An unlimited supply. (claps hands)

    (MUSIC 43. Enter 1st CHORUS GIRL L., dressed as slave girl, carrying
    tray of jewels which she places at EMPEROR's feet, salaams and backs
    away to L.)

EMPEROR:)
PING:)   Ooh.
PONG:)

EMPRESS: The Emperor will perhaps reconsider his decision to
    behead you, but as for the other matter -

    (ALADDIN claps his hands. MUSIC 44. Enter 2nd CHORUS GIRL, as
    slave with tray of jewels, which she places at EMPEROR's feet, salaams
    and backs away to L.)

EMPEROR:)
PING:)   Ooh!
PONG:)

EMPRESS: Your proposal is possibly beginning to interest the Emperor - only beginning, mind you.

(ALADDIN claps hands. MUSIC 45. Enter 3rd CHORUS GIRL, as slave with tray of jewels from L., which she places at EMPEROR's feet, salaams and backs away to L.)

EMPEROR:)
PING:)   Ooh!
PONG:)

EMPRESS: Yes - when were you thinking of getting married?

ALADDIN: Tomorrow.

EMPRESS: Oh no, out of the question.

(ALADDIN claps hands. MUSIC 46. Enter 4th CHORUS GIRL, as slave with tray of jewels from L., which she places at EMPEROR's feet, salaams and backs away to L.)

EMPEROR:)
PING:)   OOH!
PONG:)

EMPRESS: Well, now I come to think of it, we haven't anything particular on tomorrow, have we, Emperor? There's only one snag. You're a commoner.

ALADDIN: Then how about a Princeship?

EMPRESS: No, I'm afraid that's one thing that's not for sale -

(ALADDIN claps hands. MUSIC 47. Enter 5th and 6th CHORUS GIRLS, as slaves with trays of jewels from L., which they place at EMPEROR's feet and salaam.)

EMPEROR:)
PING:)   OOH!
PONG:)

EMPRESS: Usually. Even so, it's establishing a precedent.

ALADDIN: I'll throw in the slaves as well.

EMPEROR: (leaping up) Done!

(EMPEROR seizes PONG's truncheon, indicates to ALADDIN to kneel and dubs him on shoulder.)

Arise, sir Prince! Ah.

(EMPRESS rises wrathfully.)

Er - did you say something, my dear?

EMPRESS: No, but I shall have a very great deal to say later. (stalks off R.)

EMPEROR: Yes. Oh well, never mind. Now you two go and give orders for the wedding preparations to commence. Oh - and take care

EMPEROR: (continued) of the valuables too.

PING: Certainly, Emperor, certainly. Come along, my dears.

(He starts to take CHORUS GIRLS off to R.)

EMPEROR: No, no. Just show the most valuable valuables to the ante-room. I'll attend to them later.

PING: (disappointed) Yes, Emperor.

(He herds the GIRLS off L., and then returns to help PONG who is loading the jewels onto the throne.)

EMPEROR: (to ALADDIN) Talking of valuables, you seem to have so many I can't help wondering why you wear that old lamp?

ALADDIN: It's - it's a sort of family heirloom.

EMPEROR: Um - doesn't seem a very suitable ornament for a Prince. (moving towards throne, without looking at it) And that reminds me. You have a palace, of course?

(Starts to sit, PING and PONG have just moved throne and are carrying it off R. EMPEROR falls.)

ALADDIN: Of course.

EMPEROR: With furniture? (rises)

ALADDIN: Oh, yes, come and see it this afternoon and have some tea.

EMPEROR: A delightful idea. And now, I hope you don't have to rush away, because I've got a special treat for you - I'm going to sing.

ALADDIN: (backing away) Well, as a matter of fact, there are one or two things I must see about, so if you'll excuse me - (exits hurriedly L.)

EMPEROR: Beast. (to AUDIENCE) Anyway, you can't escape. I've had all the doors locked.

(Close traverse tabs slowly during number. Fly out cloth.)

MUSIC 48.   "EMPEROR'S SONG"

I am the Emperor
With umpteen Emperors before me.
Although my power is quite immense,
I'll tell you in strict confidence,
The tasks of Emperoring bore me.

Ha ha ha, ho ho ho,
Fiddle-di-dee, and hey nonny-no.
Boop-a-doop and vo-deo-do -
The tasks of Emperoring bore me.

I am the Emperor
A line I've sung to you already.
Though many Empresses there were
The last was an all-in wrestler,

EMPEROR: (continued)
And since then I've been going steady.

Hi hi hi, lo lo lo,
Fa-la-la-la, and go man go.
Yeah yeah yeah, woe woe woe,
Since then I've been going steady.

I am the Emperor
As some discover to their sorrow.
With nineteen verses more to give
I'll use my royal prerogative
And do the rest of them tomorrow.

This is my little dance,
Watch it while you have the chance,
Book your seats in advance,
I'll do the rest of it tomorrow.

(BLACKOUT.)

MUSIC 49.

Scene Nine - ABANAZAR'S DEN

(TABS. Green spot fades in L. Enter ABANAZAR L., holding crystal.)

ABANAZAR: (looking in crystal) May every scourge that ever was fall upon Aladdin's head. The wretch has discovered the lamp's secret and escaped the cave. Now a palace is to be his home and a Princess his bride. But I know a ruse will foil him yet. His palace shall scarce be built 'ere I will take it from him - aye, and his bride-to-be. But best of all I'll take the lamp! And while I'm here I might as well take this bamboo shoot.

(AUDIENCE shout. WISHEE pokes head through C. of tabs.)

WISHEE: Oi.

ABANAZAR: Curses, foiled again!

(BLACKOUT.)

(MUSIC 50. Open traverse tabs.)

Scene Ten - ALADDIN'S PALACE

(Full set. Sumptuous decor. Cut-out ground-row at back of rostrum
showing view of Pekin through windows. Balustrade along front of
rostrum steps down in C. Wing L., and wing R. SLAVE OF LAMP
discovered C. CHORUS enter in procession on rostrum leading on
ALADDIN. They process down steps and bow themselves off backwards
L. and R., as ALADDIN comes down steps.)

S. OF LAMP: Behold thy palace, lord, I pray
Doth please thee well, sire?

ALADDIN: Whew! I'll say!

(PING and PONG, now dressed as flunkeys, enter from L. and R., on
rostrum.)

S. OF LAMP: Then now 'twere best I disappear,
For lo - your guests for tea are here. (exits R.)

PING: Her Serene Highness Princess Baldroubadour.

PONG: Her Distraught Lowness Widow Twankey.

PING: His Detergentness Mr Wishee Washee.

PONG: Her Animalness Miss Typhoo.

BOTH: And their Illustrious Majesties the Emperor and Empress.

(MUSIC 51. Fanfare. Pause, while nobody appears.)

PONG: Hasn't it gone quiet all of a sudden?

(EMPEROR, EMPRESS, BALDROUBADOUR, WISHEE, TWANKEY and
TYPHOO enter at back of auditorium.)

TWANKEY: Here we are, dears.

PING: But we were expecting you to come in up here, what are
you doing down there?

EMPEROR: This is where everybody else comes in.

EMPRESS: Wherever it is, it's very dark.

TWANKEY: Yes, I think it must be the coalhole. (to one of the
AUDIENCE) Excuse me, are you a lump of coal? (HOUSE LIGHTS UP)
Oh no, how silly of me! You're much too well dressed to be a lump of
coal.

(TYPHOO has gone ahead and sat on a seat on somebody's lap near the
front.)

Oh, Wishee, just look what that naughty Typhoo's doing.

WISHEE: Oh yes, what a good idea. (joins her)

EMPRESS: Mr Wishee, kindly behave with a little more decorum.

PING: I say, I should hurry up and get up here, if I was you 'cos
we're going to get the eats in a minute.

EMPRESS: Then you can help us up first.

(PING and PONG and ALADDIN help BALDROUBADOUR, TYPHOO, EMPRESS and EMPEROR over catwalk onto stage, while TWANKEY and WISHEE continue to ad lib with AUDIENCE. PING and PONG exit L.)

TWANKEY: Come on, Wishee, let's go and get some tea.

(WISHEE crosses catwalk and TWANKEY follows hoisting up her skirts and displaying a good deal of her underwear. She looks round in pained surprise at AUDIENCE and turns round to see what has affected them. Realising what it is she turns back to them and speaks to gallery or back of auditorium.)

Put your opera glasses away.

(With great dignity she continues her journey onto stage. EMPEROR is D.R., EMPRESS D.L. Enter PING L. with a chair, which he places D.C.)

PING: Could only find one chair. (exit C.L.)

(TWANKEY produces small starter's pistol from her reticule and points it in air, drum roll, EMPEROR and EMPRESS crouch in runner's starting positions, TWANKEY fires, EMPEROR and EMPRESS run for chair, collide on it and fall on either side.)

TWANKEY: Oh well, if you two prefer the floor. (sitting) I'll have it.

EMPRESS: Mrs Twankey, how dare you sit before your Emperor and Empress have sat?

TWANKEY: Well, you are sitting, aren't you?

EMPRESS: I mean on seats.

TWANKEY: If you're not sitting on seats, what are you sitting on?

(PING and PONG run on L. with a long bench.)

PING:)
PONG:)   Look out!

(TWANKEY, clutching the chair, runs to R.C. PING and PONG put bench down L.C. and exit L. EMPEROR and EMPRESS dash for bench, EMPRESS sliding along and knocking EMPEROR off. OTHERS have moved down and now all sit down on bench in order from R. to L.: WISHEE, TYPHOO, BALDROUBADOUR, ALADDIN, EMPRESS and EMPEROR. PING enters L., holding his hands behind his back.)

EMPRESS: Now, what are we going to have?

PING: Some coffee.

EMPRESS: Coffee? But we were invited to tea.

PING: Can't help that. There's only coffee.

ALADDIN: (to EMPRESS) So sorry. (to PING) How soon can we have it then?

PING: At once.

WISHEE: Ah, instant coffee.

PING: No, Espresso.

(He blows the whistle and waves the little green flag he has been conceal-
ing behind his back and PONG enters L. "chuff-chuffing" and carrying,
so as to cover himself, a cut-out of a steam engine and pulling behind
himself a trolley with a prop espresso machine with three handles which
he pulls to a stop in front of TWANKEY. She uncouples the trolley and
he exits "chuff-chuffing" D. R. PING exits L.)

TWANKEY: Oh I've always wanted to have a go at one of these. I
wonder how you work them?

WISHEE: (moving to L. of machine) You just hold a cup under that
little spout there (points to rear of machine) and pull the handle.

TWANKEY: Oh - just like being back at the (local pub). Here goes then.

(She pulls on the L. handle and a stream of water squirts into WISHEE's
face from a concealed soda syphon with tubing to L. of machine which
TWANKEY works with her free hand out of sight behind machine.
TWANKEY though does not notice what is happening.)

There's nothing coming through yet.

WISHEE: I think perhaps you're standing in the wrong place. Try
working it from here.

(He moves round front to R. of machine, she moves to his position and
pulls down handle again and operates soda syphon with tubing to R. with
her concealed hand to squirt WISHEE.)

TWANKEY: There's still nothing coming through.

WISHEE: (mopping his face) That's what you think. Try one of the
other handles.

(She moves behind machine and pulls on centre handle pumping it like a
beer engine.)

TWANKEY: Oh, yes. This better. It's coming through beautifully
now. Yes, there we are.

(She holds up a full glass of beer. The beer is set in a jug which she
pours into the glass with her concealed hand.)

Oh, a lovely drop of cappuchino that.

WISHEE: I think I'd like a cup of that too.

OTHERS: And me!

(TYPHOO holds up her hand eagerly.)

TWANKEY: Righto. (She pulls on C. handle again, evidently from
the way she continues pulling, without success.) Oh dear. What a pity.
It seems to have run out.

(OTHERS all groan.)

TWANKEY:	(continued) Never mind. I've got another handle left. (she pulls on it - it comes off in her hand.) I <u>had</u> another handle left. (throws handle off stage) I'm afraid you've had the coffee.

(OTHERS groan again. WISHEE disappointedly pushes trolley off D.R.)

EMPRESS:	How very provoking.

ALADDIN:	Never mind. I'm sure we can have something to eat.

(TYPHOO rubs her tummy eagerly.)

PONG:	(runs on R., with a plate of sausage rolls one of which disguises a small pistol) Here you are. Banger rolls. Who wants a banger roll?

PRINCESS B:	What's a banger roll?

PONG:	A roll what goes bang. (fires pistol)

(He runs off L. to TYPHOO's disappointment. She tries to take one of them as he passes but is too late. PING runs on D.L. with a plate of cakes.)

PING:	Rock cakes. Who wants a rock cake?

(TYPHOO rubs her tummy.)

EMPEROR:	What kind of rock?

PING:	Solid rock.

(Hits EMPEROR on head with one, he rolls off bench and rolls away.)

EMPRESS:	Ah, rock and roll.

(She is vastly amused by her own joke, but none of the others are. She stops when she notices this.)

Emperor, what is the penalty for not laughing at royal jokes?

EMPEROR:	(rubbing his own pate sorrowfully) Beheading.

OTHERS:	Beheading? (They all laugh falsely but loudly and abruptly stop)

EMPRESS:	That's better.

(PING runs off L. TYPHOO is again disappointed and unable to snatch one before he exits.)

TWANKEY:	Isn't there anything else to eat?

PONG:	(running on L. holding a plate with Christmas pudding on it) Yes. Christmas pud.

OTHERS:	Ah!

PONG:	Oops!

(He trips and drops pudding. It bounces (covered ball). TYPHOO catches it and runs off R. with it.)

WISHEE:	That means we've had the pudding.
PONG:	That's a pity because there isn't anything else. (exits L.)
ALADDIN:	It looks as if we'" just have to sing for our supper.
PRINCESS B:	Sing a song?

(PING and PONG run on L., with music sheets concealed behind their backs.)

PING:) PONG:)	You called?
ALADDIN:	No, we want to sing a song.
PING:) PONG:)	(producing music) Of sixpence?
TWANKEY:	No, of sevenpence.
PING:) PONG:)	(distributing music) Of sixpence. Sevenpence doesn't scan.

(CHORUS can enter for number, if desired.)

MUSIC 52. "SING A SONG OF SIXPENCE" (in the manner of Handel.)

ALL:
Sing a song, sing a song of sixpence - of sixpence,
A pocketful of rye.
Four and twenty blackbirds,
Four and twenty blackbirds,
Four and twenty blackbirds,
Four and twenty blackbirds,
    Baked in a pie.

(Repeat.)

But when the pie was opened,
The birds began to sing,
Wasn't that a dainty dish to set before the King?
Wasn't that a dainty dish?
Wasn't that a dainty dish?
Wasn't that a dainty dish to set before the King?

Sing a song, sing a song of sixpence,
    Of sixpence,
Sing a song, sing a song of -
Sing a song, sing a song of -
Sing a song, sing a song of - sixpence!

(PING and PONG collect up music and exit L.)

EMPRESS:	Excellent. Now, Aladdin, as you're getting married tomorrow I think you'd better have a stag party.
ALADDIN:	Oh, certainly. Just the Emperor and Wishee and me, you mean?
EMPRESS:	And me.

ALADDIN: But, your Majesty you're not a stag, you're a doe.

EMPRESS: Oh, doe I'm not.   (laughs heartily at her pun until she realises that again nobody is with her.)   That was another royal joke.

(ALL laugh heartily and falsely again and abruptly stop.)

Thank you. Come along then. Oh, but first take that dirty old lamp off. You can't take me out wearing a thing like that.

ALADDIN: Oh, but I couldn't.

EMPRESS: Of course you could.   Leave it here.

PRINCESS B: I'll look after it for you, darling.

(ALADDIN reluctantly gives lamp to PRINCESS BALDROUBADOUR.)

EMPRESS: That's right. Emperor, hurry up and say goodbye.

EMPEROR: Oh yes. Goodbye.   (shakes hands with BALDROUBADOUR.)

PRINCESS B: Goodbye.

EMPEROR: Goodbye. Are you sure you have to leave so soon?

PRINCESS B: I'm not going.

EMPEROR: But you must be, otherwise we shouldn't have said goodbye.

EMPRESS: Don't be silly, Emperor. We're the ones who are leaving.

EMPEROR: Oh, are we? In that case, I'd better say goodbye. Goodbye. (starts to wander off R.)

EMPRESS: No, no, no. Not that way, this way.

(EMPRESS, EMPEROR, WISHEE and ALADDIN exit R. on rostrum. BALDROUBADOUR and TWANKEY sit on bench.)

PRINCESS B: Mother's rather bossy, I'm afraid. I hope I'm not like that with Aladdin, I do so want to be a good wife. But I'm afraid I don't know much about housework. Could you teach me?

TWANKEY: Oh yes, dear. Washing's my speciality. I could give you a lesson in that right now if I nipped back to the laundry and got some things.

PRINCESS B: Oh yes, please, and cooking too. Could you teach me how to cook?

TWANKEY: Well, I'll give you my favourite recipe.

MUSIC 53. "RECIPE" (Words & music by John Crocker, arr., Eric Gilder)

Take two lips,
Then take two more,
And mix them well together.
Stir with bliss
To make a kiss,
As sweet as honey heather.

Take two hearts
To make a pair,

TWANKEY: (continued)
> Both with joy a-singing.
> Soon you'll find
> That you're inclined
> To wedding bells a-ringing.
>
> Take a pair
> And soon there's three,
> With baby clothes and nappies out a-drying.
> Out of key
> The harmony
> When baby starts a-crying.
>
> Take some love
> And give it all
> And all your life keep giving
> Then you'll bake
> Life's richest cake
> For love's the spice of living.   (exits L.)

PRINCESS B: How splendid to have such a helpful mother-in-law. And I do want to be a thrifty housewife, but it's rather difficult when you're not brought up to that sort of thing.

ABANAZAR: (off R. In disguised voice) New lamps for old! New lamps for old! Bring me your old lamps and I will give you new ones.

PRINCESS B: (running up to window) What's that?

ABANAZAR: (off) New lamps for old!

PRINCESS B: It's an old pedlar. Oh, what a splendid chance for me to practice a little thriftiness with this old lamp of Aladdin's. (calling off) Hi, pedlar! Come up here. I've got an old lamp for you.

ABANAZAR: (off) Coming, my dear, coming.

PRINCESS B: I wonder why the old man wants to give away new lamps? Still, that's his business and it's very lucky for me. Aladdin will be pleased.

(Enter ABANAZAR R., on rostrum, disguised as a Pedlar with a tray of lamps.)

ABANAZAR: Here I am, my dear.

PRINCESS B: Will you exchange this lamp, pedlar? I'm afraid it's a very old one.

ABANAZAR: Never mind. I care not how old. Give it me and you shall have this shining new one.

(They exchange lamps.)

At last! At last! (rubs lamp)

(Cymbal roll and crash, blue flame. MUSIC 54. SLAVE OF LAMP enters. PRINCESS BALDROUBADOUR shrinks back terrified.)

S. OF LAMP: My master calls and I am here.

ABANAZAR: Then list, while I my needs make clear.
                           This palace must transported be
                           To Africa, immediately!

S. OF LAMP: My lord commands, it shall be done,
                           With speed as swift as shot from gun!

(SLAVE OF LAMP makes magic pass - EFFECT 34 - thunder, lightning.
EFFECT 35 - wind noise -)

(BLACKOUT.)

(MUSIC 55. Fly in Scene Eleven cloth or close traverse tabs and set
notice board.)

Scene Eleven - OUTSIDE THE PALACE

(Frontcloth showing open space with notice in middle - "DESIRABLE BUILDING SITE FOR SALE", or tabs with similarly worded noticeboard C. Two hooks in cloth or on board. Enter TWANKEY L., followed by TYPHOO carrying laundry.)

TWANKEY: Now where's that palace got to, Typhoo? I thought it was along here. (sees notice) Well, it can't be, can it? I say, you seem to have got some very peculiar laundry for Baldroubadour. (takes pyjama trousers from TYPHOO) Just look at these pyjama trousers - there's music written all over them.

(TYPHOO nods and points to jacket.)

What's that? Something written on the jacket, too? (takes jacket) Ooh, what a huge jacket it is. Oh yes, there's some words here. Well, the two of them together must make a song. Let's hear what it sounds like, eh?

(TYPHOO agrees.)

Here, (conductor's name), run over this for us, will you?

(Throws pyjama trousers into pit and ORCHESTRA play a few bars of song sheet.)

Oh yes, that's very pretty. Now let's see if the words fit. Oh - where can I hang the jacket, Typhoo?

(TYPHOO looks around then sees hooks and points to them.)

Oh yes, two hooks. What a bit of luck.

(They hang jacket on hooks.)

That's it. Now, give me a chord to start.

(CONDUCTOR throws up pyjama cord.)

Not the pyjama cord, silly. A musical chord.

(The ORCHESTRA oblige.)

Oh yes, that one's just my size.

MUSIC 56. "PANDA PUZZLE"

> I know mices come in different sizes;
> I know an elephant is grander;
> I know gnus and kangaroos -
> But I'll never understand a panda!

(TYPHOO applauds vigorously.)

Oh, a very pretty ditty. (notices TYPHOO) Well, you're applauding so much I think you must have written it.

(TYPHOO admits it and then becomes very shy.)

Oh, it's all right, dear. I won't tell anybody, but I tell you what I will do - I'll ask all of them to sing it with us. That'll be a big surprise for them, won't it?

(TYPHOO shakes head)

TWANKEY: (continued) No? Well, they'll be all the more ready to sing it then. (ad lib with AUDIENCE for song sheet) Well, I'm afraid that's all we've got time for now.

(CONDUCTOR throws pyjama trousers up.)

What's the matter - don't they fit you? I think you'd better take these back and get me some laundry without anything written on it, Typhoo.

(TYPHOO nods and runs off L. with laundry.)

And I must see if I can find Aladdin's palace.

(Enter ALADDIN, WISHEE, EMPEROR and EMPRESS R.)

EMPRESS: Oh, Emperor, how careless of you to have lost the way.

EMPEROR: Well, I know I had it when we started, my dear.

TWANKEY: Oh, Aladdin dear, how fortunate. I can't find your palace.

ALADDIN: Don't be silly, mother, you're standing right outside it. (turns) No - no - what's happened? It's gone! The entire palace gone!

EMPRESS: What's this? The palace gone! Then what's happened to our daughter?

TWANKEY: That's all right. I left Baldroubadour in the palace. (Realising.) In the palace!

EMPRESS: Perfidious youth! You have spirited her away. Return her immediately, or we really will have you beheaded.

ALADDIN: Oh, mother, what can I do?

TWANKEY: I know, dear, just rub the lamp.

ALADDIN: The lamp! That was in the palace too! Oh! I'm ruined!

WISHEE: I don't know - you might raise a few bob on that ring.

ALADDIN: (rubbing hands together in agitation) This? No it's worthless, worthless.

(Red flash, cymbal roll and crash. MUSIC 57. SLAVE OF RING enters L. (or through C., if tabs). Close traverse tabs slowly and fly out cloth.)

S. OF RING: (salaams) Master, most dread, most august sire,
Command thy slave what dost desire;
For whosoever wears the ring
Him will I serve in ev'rything.

ALADDIN: What's this? The ring is magic too?
What luck! Now, if you only knew
Just where my love and palace are.

S. OF RING: I do, my lord. In Africa.

ALADDIN: Then instantly return them here.

S. OF RING: That, master, cannot be, I fear;

S. OF RING: (continued) They are protected by the lamp
     Which Abanazar has.

TWANKEY: The scamp!

S. OF RING: To fight the lamp I must not dare.
     But I could swiftly take thee there.

ALADDIN: Then let's be gone without delay.

S. OF RING: (salaams) Master, I hear and I obey.

 (Cymbals crash, EFFECT 36 thunder roll, lightning, EFFECT 37 wind noises.)

 (BLACKOUT.)

MUSIC 58.

 (Open traverse tabs.)

Scene Twelve - THE PALACE, AFRICA

(Set as for Scene Ten, but with cut-out ground-rows of African view
through windows at back. A couch L. C. with small table beside it.
Five goblets on table. CHORUS discovered as Eastern dancers,
ABANAZAR and PRINCESS BALDROUBADOUR seated on couch.
MUSIC 59. CHORUS perform eastern dance and exit at end of it.)

ABANAZAR: Did that entertainment please my fair lotus blossom?

PRINCESS B: No. And I'm not a lotus blossom.

ABANAZAR: True - thou hast the rarer beauty of a desert flower. Ah!
How my heart burns for thee!

PRINCESS B: Well, if you've got heartburn, you'd better take some
bicarb.

ABANAZAR: My precious rosebud still has angry thorns, I see.

PRINCESS B: First a lotus blossom, then a desert flower, now a rosebud. You seem to think I'm a herbaceous border.

ABANAZAR: No, no. I think thee a most lovely woman whom I dearly
wish to call my own. Come, can you not like me a little?

PRINCESS B: No, I think you're the most revolting person I've ever met.

ABANAZAR: Doubtless time will bring a change. (rising) Perhaps if I
prepare thee a refreshing drink, cunningly spiced and fragr: it with rose
leaves, 'twill incline thee more kindly toward me. (exits U. .:. on
rostrum)

PRINCESS B: If it has any of that disgusting sherbet in it, it won't.
(rising and coming to C.) Oh dear. I would have to try to be thrifty
wouldn't I? If ever I get back to Aladdin I'll be the most extravagant wife
there ever was. If I get back, that is. Never mind, however far apart
we may be, my heart will be with him always.

MUSIC 60. "CONSTANT LOVE"

> I have a heart that is shaped like a prison;
> I have a key that's hidden away.
> There I have locked all my love for safe-keeping
> Till my true love returns some fine day.
> I have my eyes on the distant horizon,
> I have my dreams in faraway lands.
> There they will stay till my love is beside me,
> Till I can place my heart in his hands.
> Deserts and mountains and seas may divide us -
> He may have journeyed to regions unknown.
> Time has no meaning while here I am waiting -
> He is my love and I am his own.
> Here I will wait till the dawning of never,
> Till all the breath of life shall depart,
> Till he sets free all the love locked within me,
> Here prisoned in my heart.

(Exit PRINCESS BALDROUBADOUR L. Slight pause. WISHEE's head topped with a fez and heavily but very obviously falsely bearded pokes round D. R. wing. ALADDIN's head similarly treated pokes round on top of his. WISHEE having had a good look round, nods, turns back and both are taken by surprise.)

ALADDIN:)
WISHEE:)   Aah! (They recover. Severely to each other) Ssh!

(WISHEE creeps onstage to reveal a long tight-fitting Egyptian robe. He beckons to ALADDIN, who follows him on similarly dressed and dragging a rope behind him and they both beckon to off R. Nothing happens.)

ALADDIN: Come on, mother.

(He pulls on the rope and obviously meets with some resistance at the other end. WISHEE comes to his aid.)

WISHEE: Come on, Mrs Twankey.

(MUSIC 61. They heave and drag on a reluctant CAMEL. TWANKEY follows wearing a rather odd Eastern costume. The face is veiled by a yashmak and through her transparent Eastern trousers can be seen her red flannel bloomers, her ringed stockings and her elastic sided boots.)

TWANKEY: Whoa!

(The CAMEL stops and TWANKEY pulls a string and the yashmak draws back like a curtain. CAMEL turns head to look at her.)

Don't you look at me like that - you and your two humps.   (rubs behind painfully)

(CAMEL yawns hugely and kneels on its forelegs. The rear slowly slides down so that its legs are alongside front, then with right leg scratches itself. It closes its eyes. ALADDIN and WISHEE take off their beards.)

ALADDIN: I think we were very lucky to find him when we fell off that cloud.

TWANKEY: Yes, but I think that slave of the ring should have given us a bigger one. I mean five of us on a minicloud - it's ridiculous.

ALADDIN: The Emperor and Empress must still be on it. I wonder what's happened to them?

WISHEE: With the Emperor steering I should think they're just about over Iceland now.

TWANKEY: Aye aye, Old Rip van Winkle's dropped off again.

ALADDIN: Then we'd better wake him and get him out of here.

TWANKEY: Yes, he is a bit sort of obvious.

ALL THREE: Wakee, wakee, Ripee, Ripee!

(CAMEL remains oblivious.)

WISHEE: We'll just have to lift him up.

(They bend their efforts to this and get the rear half up.)

TWANKEY: We're getting on, now the other bit.

(They move to his front and get that up. Immediately the rear half goes down again. They run to the rear and get that up again and the front goes down.)

WISHEE: Well, I'll hold this while you pull the front up.

(TWANKEY and ALADDIN go and pull the front up. The rear forces down so that WISHEE ends up underneath it.)

Help!

TWANKEY: Coming! Hold this!

(ALADDIN holds the front up. TWANKEY goes and lifts the rear. The front goes down with ALADDIN underneath it, and before TWANKEY can stop it the rear collapses with both herself and WISHEE underneath.)

ALADDIN: Now what are we going to do?

(CAMEL yawns, looks around, slowly rises and daintily steps backward off them then kneels with forelegs and slides down with back legs as before.)

ALL: Oh, Rip.

ABANAZAR: (off R.) Your sherbet, my love.

ALL: Abanazar!

WISHEE: Skedaddle!

(They rise hastily putting on beards and drawing yashmak hastily.)

ABANAZAR: (off R. singing) Sherbet for two, and two for sherbet.

(They run off to L., falling over couch as they do so. ABANAZAR enters R., on rostrum carrying a large gold jug.)

Sherbet for two - (looks over balustrade) Ah, not here, (moving on) and two for sherbet.

(He exits L., on rostrum. OTHERS start to come on. ABANAZAR returns from L., and stops and looks at CAMEL as they rush off again.)

Strange, I don't remember ordering a camel.

(Turns and exits L., on rostrum. The OTHERS come on again taking off beards and drawing yashmak.)

ALL THREE: Whew!

ALADDIN: Now, we must find Baldroubadour.

TWANKEY: Yes, and quickly too, before old Abernasty turns up again.

ALADDIN: Then let's split up. We'll go this way, Mother. You go that way, Wishee.

(ALADDIN and TWANKEY hurry off D. L.)

WISHEE: But I'm all by myself. Oh well, I don't mind. (goes a few paces to R.) Would you like to come with me, Rip?

(CAMEL shakes his head.)

Coward. (goes reluctantly off D.R.)

(CAMEL looks round and sees bamboo shoot, stands up, looks to L. and R., does a little hop with its front legs, a little hop with its rear legs then trots over to shoot. AUDIENCE shout. CAMEL jumps back and rear half jumps up onto front half pigabackwise and runs U.L., to stop in front of couch facing R., then resumes normal standing posture. WISHEE runs on R.)

Right, coming thank you. (pulls up seeing nobody there) Oh, who was it then? The camel? (moves to couch, waggling finger at him) You're a naughty old Rip.

(CAMEL snaps at his finger.)

Ow, don't nip, Rip.

(TWANKEY and ALADDIN run on D.L.)

ALADDIN: Quickly, I think there's somebody coming. We must get him out of here.

(ALADDIN and TWANKEY push at his hindquarters.)

TWANKEY: Come on. gideup there.

ALADDIN: He's moving!

(CAMEL front legs remain stationary and rear legs move up to them.)

TWANKEY: He's shrunk.

(CAMEL's rear legs remain stationary and front legs move forward. WISHEE is knocked down.)

WISHEE: He's difficult.

TWANKEY: Try winding him up.

(ALADDIN winds CAMEL's tail. CAMEL tosses head superciliously and lies down on couch. WISHEE rises.)

ALADDIN: Any sign of anybody yet?

WISHEE: (looking off L.) Yes!

ALADDIN: Vamoose!

(They rush upstage.)

TWANKEY: Too late.

(They freeze into imitations of eastern statuary. Enter BALDROUBA-DOUR L. She does a double take on them, they relax and move towards her. She backs away scared.)

ALADDIN: (taking BALDROUBADOUR in his arms and kissing her) My darling.

(BALDROUBADOUR shrieks.)

ALADDIN: (continued) Oh, sorry.

(He throws his beard off and TWANKEY catches it. She opens her yashmak. WISHEE takes off his beard and puts it on CAMEL.)

PRINCESS B: Aladdin! Wishee! Mrs Twankey! How did you get here?

ALADDIN: My dearest, we'll explain all that later. Abanazar may be back at any minute and he mustn't find us here. The important thing is to get hold of the lamp. Now look, here is a phial of poison. (produces phial and holds it up)

PRINCESS B: Poison! But we don't want to kill him, do we?

ALADDIN: No, but this poison won't, because he's a magician. But it will lay him out for a bit while we get the lamp. Be careful with it, though - it would kill any of us.

ABANAZAR: (off L.) Did you call, my peach bloom? Coming.

TWANKEY: Scarper!

(Instant activity. TWANKEY shoves ALADDIN's beard on herself and she, WISHEE and ALADDIN run R., till ALADDIN discovers the loss of his beard.)

ALADDIN: (in heavy whisper) My beard! Where's my beard?

WISHEE: (in heavy whisper) And mine! Where's mine?

ALADDIN: (finding beard on CAMEL) Ah!

WISHEE: (snatching it and putting it on. Heavy whisper) No, that's mine.

ALADDIN: (heavy whisper) Where's mine got to then?

(The four of them look round on floor for it.)

TWANKEY: (heavy whisper) Can't see it anywhere, dear.

PRINCESS B: (pointing at TWANKEY, heavy whisper) There.

TWANKEY: (looking behind herself. Heavy whisper) Where? (turns right round)

ALADDIN: (seeing her as she comes round) Oh, mother.

(He hurriedly snatches beard and puts it on and turns upstage to give PRINCESS BALDROUBADOUR, now on couch, a final kiss. TWANKEY draws yashmak.)

Goodbye, dear.

(WISHEE and TWANKEY pull him away to R. Beard is left on BALDROU-BADOUR. ALADDIN realises loss and pulls TWANKEY and WISHEE back to get beard. He puts it on and they are running R. again as ABANAZAR enters L. on rostrum with the jug.)

ABANAZAR: Here I am, my sweetmeat.

TWANKEY:)
ALADDIN:)   (sotto voce) Sunk.
WISHEE:)

(ABANAZAR moves quickly with arms outstretched to couch to embrace
BALDROUBADOUR, first putting jug on table. As he sits BALDROUBA-
DOUR moves away to avoid his embrace and the CAMEL turns his head
in so that ABANAZAR embraces the camel instead. He quickly disengages
in disgust.)

ABANAZAR: Who is this creature? And who are all these people?

PRINCES B: Oh - er - oh, just some - er - er - dancing dervishes.

(ALADDIN, WISHEE and TWANKEY look at each other doubtfully, then
nod ingratiatingly at ABANAZAR.)

ABANAZAR: Really? I knew not that there were female dervishes.

PRINCESS B: No. Very few. In fact - this is the only one.

ABANAZAR: And why are they here?

PRINCESS B: Well, you know how wild dervishes are. They just popped
in on impulse.

ABANAZAR: Impulse!

PRINCESS B: Yes, they - er - thought we might like to see one of
their dances.

(They shake their heads violently at her, then, seeing ABANAZAR looking
at them, nod equally violently at him.)

ABANAZAR: Excellent. They shall entertain us. (he sits on couch and
claps hands to off L.) Music for the dancers.

(MUSIC 62. ALADDIN, WISHEE and TWANKEY look at each other blankly
as Eastern music starts. Then they shrug, salaam to ABANAZAR. TWANKEY
moves to a position near ABANAZAR and her voice bursts out with a very
loud impression of a wailing Eastern chant. ALL others put their hands
to their ears and the CAMEL is especially enraged. CAMEL rises and
stalks across the stage in sniffy dignity to exit R.)

TWANKEY: Sorry.

(She starts her chant again in a more moderate voice endeavouring to
fascinate ABANAZAR with some rather inept hip swaying, etc. Meanwhile WISHEE and ALADDIN dance round and round the couch in a
somewhat angular fashion, trying from time to time to steal the lamp,
which ABANAZAR has attached to a cord round his neck. At the end of
the dance TWANKEY does such an elaborate salaam that she falls over
and ABANAZAR rises to help her up.)

ALADDIN: (to BALDROUBADOUR) Quick! The poison!

(They pour some poison into one of the goblets.)

ABANAZAR: Splendid. Now, you must drink with us and refresh
yourselves.

(He hands TWANKEY the poisoned goblet, which she is just about to gulp down.

PRINCESS B: (heavy whisper) No! Poison! (helps out her heavy whispering with some heavy miming.)

(TWANKEY splutters, puts goblet down and pretends to have a fit of coughing. While ALADDIN and ABANAZAR help her to get over this, BALDROUBADOUR switches the goblets so that the poisoned one is nearest to ABANAZAR.)

ABANAZAR: (presenting poisoned goblet to BALDROUBADOUR) My love, your drink.

PRINCESS B: (hastily picking up another cup) No, this was mine.

ABANAZAR: (to ALADDIN) Yours then?

ALADDIN: (taking another goblet) No this was mine.

ABANAZAR: (to WISHEE) Yours then?

WISHEE: (taking another goblet) No this was mine.

TWANKEY: It must be mine then. (takes it then hastily hands it back) No, yours.

ABANAZAR: (taking another goblet) No this was mine. (putting goblets down) I remember it stood on the table here.

PRINCESS B: (moving it) No here.

ABANAZAR: (moving it) No here.

ALADDIN: (moving it) No here.

ABANAZAR: (moving it) No here.

TWANKEY: (moving it) No here.

ABANAZAR: (moving it) No here.

WISHEE: (moving it) No here.

(They continue to change all the cups round very quickly until they don't know which is which and are stopped by ABANAZAR firmly taking up a goblet.)

ABANAZAR: Come, we will drink.

(The other four put out reluctant hands for the remaining goblets.)

ALADDIN:)   (very quickly) Eeny, meeny, miny, mo,
PRINCESS B:)   Catch a nigger by his toe,
TWANKEY:)   If he hollers let him go,
WISHEE:)   Eeny, meeny, miny, mo.

(They pick up their goblets thus chosen.)

ABANAZAR: Your health.

```
ALADDIN:    )
PRINCESS B: )
TWANKEY:    )   (politely)  Yours.
WISHEE:     )
```

(ABANAZAR drinks deeply. The other four raise their cups a little but watch attentively for results.)

ABANAZAR: Ah, delicious.

(Others look away very disappointed and gaze with great disfavour into their own goblets.)

Some more, I think. (starts to pour himself some more, then suddenly clutches stomach) Aaahhh! What's this? Are all the furies come to stir my stomach? A mighty pain holds me in its grip! I have been poisoned! Aaahhh! Twice ten thousand million cur - AAAAHHHH!

(He staggers back towards couch, then with another loud cry totters U.R. The others pick up couch and hurry over with it to place it behind him. Just as they get there he gives another howl of pain and staggers D.R. They pick up couch again and follow him down. He immediately stumbles U.L., they rush behind with the couch, he teeters almost falling back onto it, then staggers D.L. Disgusted, they plonk the couch down in its original position and fold their arms, so he is forced to stumble back to it, which he does with gathering momentum and falls heavily backwards over it, leaving only one foot showing.)

ALADDIN: Quickly! The lamp! Before he recovers.

(ALADDIN and BALDROUBADOUR bend to get it. Enter EMPEROR and EMPRESS C.R.)

EMPRESS: Emperor, that's the last time I ever travel on a cloud with you driving. Ah, just what I could do with - a nice drink. (picks up ABANAZAR's goblet from table)

TWANKEY: No! Poison!

EMPRESS: (laughingly) Poison. (is about to drink, realises) POISON! (flings goblet away and rushes across to sit on couch. Plucks ABANA-ZAR's slipper from his foot and vigorously fans herself with it) What do you mean? What's going on here? Baldroubadour, who are all these people?

(ALADDIN and WISHEE remove beards.)

PRINCESS B: Aladdin and Wishee and Mrs Twankey.

EMPEROR: (lifting up TWANKEY's yashmak) She's right, you know.

(TWANKEY draws yashmak. EMPRESS realises what she has been fanning herself with and is puzzled as to where it came from. She is surprised to find ABANAZAR's foot beside her and hastily replaces slipper.)

EMPRESS: (pointing at foot) But then who's this?

ALADDIN: He's the man who stole my magic lamp and spirited my

ALADDIN: (continued) palace away.

PRINCESS B: His name's Abanazar, and he's a very wicked magician.

EMPEROR: A magician! Oh, I say, how wizard!

(TWANKEY and WISHEE shake their heads at each other and hold their noses.)

I've always wanted a court magician.

ABANAZAR: AH!

(He recovers violently, coming up on to couch, which gives EMPRESS such a jump that she falls off. TWANKEY jumps up on to WISHEE, who is barely able to support her.)

So! 'Twas you Aladdin. You have foiled me once again and all my plans are come to naught.

TWANKEY: (crossing to couch and patting him on head) Never mind, dear. The Emperor's got a nice job for you, and I've got one or two plans for you myself.

ABANAZAR: (takes on her) Pass the poison.

EMPRESS: (rising) I suppose there's no reason for Aladdin to be beheaded now. How unfortunate, I was so looking forward to it.

EMPEROR: Never mind my dear, let's get back to China and get on with the wedding instead.

ALADDIN: (preparing to rub lamp) That's very quickly done.

TWANKEY: (pouncing on couch and knocking ABANAZAR off onto floor) Bags the sofa for the journey.

(ALADDIN rubs lamp. Cymbal roll and crash, blue flash. MUSIC 63. Enter SLAVE OF LAMP R.)

S. OF LAMP: My master calls and I am here.

ALADDIN: Then through the air the palace steer
                      And let us home to Pekin go!

S. OF LAMP: My lord commands, it shall be so!

(EFFECT 38 Thunder, lightning -)

(BLACKOUT and EFFECT 39 wind noises.)

MUSIC 64.

(Close traverse tabs.)

Scene Thirteen - LOST PROPERTY

(Tabs or frontcloth. A street. (Scene Two cloth could be used again.))

PING: (off L.) Oi, come back!

(TYPHOO scoots on from L. , on PING's scooter and off R.)

(off L.) Come back! Wait! Stop! Stop!

(As she goes off R. , PING runs on L. , and as he continues across stage she returns on scooter from R. , head down and buffets into him, knocking him over.)

Oooof! (he rises, winded, trying to get his breath back)

PONG: (shouting off R.) Oi, come back! Come back!

(At the same moment the CAMEL enters R. , on PONG's scooter. (I would suggest in its closed up position with the front half gripping the handlebars through the skin so that it looks as if the neck is resting on the handlebars.) It bumps into PING knocking him over onto his face. PONG runs on R. , after it.)

Oh dear.

(CAMEL gets off scooter letting it fall and backing away. PONG moves in to pick it up, while PING rises, winded again, and gesticulating violently at PONG.)

PING: What do you mean - running into me like that?

PONG: I didn't. (points to CAMEL) He did.

(CAMEL tries to look aloof.)

PING: Who's he then?

PONG: Lost property.

PING: Really? This is lost property too.

PONG: Funny, they don't look alike. (to TYPHOO) Perhaps we'd better introduce 'em. Lost property, meet lost property. (to CAMEL) Lost property, this is lost property.

(TYPHOO and CAMEL are rather shy about each other.)

PING: Well, go on, say how do you do.

(TYPHOO gives a little bob of a curtsey and looks hastily away.)

(CAMEL gives a quick little bow and looks hastily away.)

PING: No, no, no. Say how do you do properly.

(TYPHOO gives a maidenly wriggle.)   ) to-

(CAMEL kicks one foot with the other in boyish embarrassment.)) gether

PING: Oh, go on. Shake feet.

(TYPHOO coyly skips over to CAMEL and they shake a forepaw and a foreleg.)

PING: I can see Wishee's going to have to take on another animal when he turns up again. Meanwhile, you must remember that you're lost property and behave as lost property.

(CAMEL and TYPHOO nod.)

Lost property does not ride on scooters.

(CAMEL and TYPHOO shake heads.)

Supposing we hadn't found you? Where would you have been then?

(CAMEL and TYPHOO exchange looks then TYPHOO shrugs.)

Exactly. Lost. And what's the use of lost property that you can't find?

(CAMEL and TYPHOO shake heads.)

(to PONG) Well, you tell 'em.

PONG: I can't. I'm lost for words.

PING: And I've lost the thread of what I was saying.

PING:)
PONG:)   So now, we're all lost.

MUSIC 65. "LOST"

How do people come to lose a camel?
A camel's not a thing you can mislay.
    It clutters up the floor;
    You can't leave it in a drawer;
You don't see homeless camels every day.
Despite it's very self-effacing manner,
    The desert ship is quite a biggish craft.
How do people come to lose a camel?
    It's just plain daft!

How do people come to lose a Panda?
A Panda's quite a tricky thing to lose.
    It's not a thing one sees
    Hanging round in all the trees;
One only finds them in the best of Zoos.
It's just the sort of thing that people notice,
    A funny looking thing both fore and aft.
How do people come to lose a Panda?
    It's just plain daft!

How do people come to lose two policemen?
They rarely ever wander from their beat.
    Though they disguise themselves
    As fairies or as elves,
You'd know them by their size eleven feet!
The only other time that we were missing,
    The police Inspector laughed and laughed and
        laughed,
How do people come to lose two policemen?
    It's just plain daft!

MUSIC 66. "MAKE WAY" reprise

(CHORUS enter L. moving across stage. Traverse tabs open behind them on last few bars.)

CHORUS:
                    Make way, oh, make way,
                        Wedding time is here.
                    Make way, oh, make way
                      See the streets are clear
                For our royal couple we must all make way,
              Make way, make way, make way, it's their wedding
                                      day.

(CHORUS exit L. and R. on last line, music continues for walk down.)

Scene Fourteen - ALADDIN'S WEDDING
BANQUET

(The palace with Chinese view through windows again, or another more
sumptuous set. CHORUS enter from L and R on rostrum, in pairs. Each
pair meets in C. of rostrum and comes D.C., to take their bow. They
then split and back away to form diagonal lines L. and R. The principals
follow a similar procedure, forming diagonal lines in front of CHORUS.
SLAVE OF LAMP from R., backing R. and SLAVE OF RING from L.,
backing L: CAMEL from R., backing R: PING from R., backing R. and
PONG from L., backing R.: EMPRESS from R., backing L., and
EMPEROR from L., backing L.: TYPHOO from R., backing R.:
ABANAZAR from L., backing L.: WISHEE from R., backing R.:
TWANKEY from L., backing L. MUSIC 67. Fanfare. ALL turn in as
BALDROUBADOUR enters from R. and ALADDIN from L. and meet in
C. of rostrum.)

ALL: Hurray!

(ALADDIN and BALDROUBADOUR move D.C. to take their bow.
Principals move down into a straight line with them. CHORUS move up
onto rostrum.)

ALADDIN: Our tale has nothing more to tell,
                  All's ended happily and well.
                  I have the lamp and - which is more -
                  My fair Princess Baldroubadour.

PRINCESS B: I Aladdin won, lost, and won,
                  Which, all in all, was rather fun.

WISHEE: And I at last to dear Typhoo
                  Can give this shoot of sweet bamboo.
                  (gives her part of bamboo plant)

ALADDIN: So, but remains 'ere you do go
                  (bowing to CONDUCTOR)
                  To play the tune that ends our show.

CONDUCTOR: My lord commands, it shall be so.

    MUSIC 68. FINALE ("MAKE WAY" Reprise)

                  Make way oh make way,
                      Here comes happiness,
                  For Prince Aladdin and his sweet Princess.
                  Make way, oh make way,
                      Though our tale is done,
                  For the royal couple it has just begun.

    (CURTAIN)

FURNITURE AND PROPERTY PLOT

Set on stage throughout: Large flower pot in front of L., proscenium arch with bamboo plant to grow out of it. (i.e. pulled up on thin nylon line attached to it and threaded offstage.)

Scene One

OFF R.

Scooter labelled "POLICE" with prop handmike on handlebars.	PING
Two large maces	PING & PONG
Scroll	EMPEROR
Old chairpram, fitted with mock engine on back, hooter on handle and pile of washing on seat.	TWANKEY
Umbrella	TWANKEY
Manacle chains	PING & PONG

OFF L.

Scooter labelled "POLICE" with prop handmike on handlebars	PONG
Collar and leash	TYPHOO
Three bamboo shoots	WISHEE
Large notice "POISON"	WISHEE
Cushion with large sponge on it	1st CHORUS
Cushion with loofah	2nd CHORUS
Large bath towel and salver with tin of talcum powder and large tablet of soap	3rd CHORUS
Salver with perfume spray	4th CHORUS
Canopy	5th & 6th CHORUS

PERSONAL

PING	Notebook, whistle, truncheon.
PONG	Truncheon.
TWANKEY	Handkerchief.

Scene Two

Set on stage: A covered crystal ball R.
A casket containing ring C.

OFF L.

Two bags of gold	ABANAZAR

Scene Three

Set on stage:
Small rug in front of D. L. opening.
Kitchen range set in front of R. wing.
Doll's baby jacket in oven.
Plate rack above range.
Breakable plates in rack. (These can be made from old 78 records, shaped by softening them in an oven, then moulding them on a plate and painting. Administered with a sharp tap, they are quite harmless.)
Prop poker with red painted end on range.
Large bucket D. S. of range.
Framed picture (picture made of paper perforated in a star shape in the middle to break easily) and comic telephone set on cut-out at C. back.
Small shopping bag and TYPHOO's lead on cupboard door.
Table C. with upright chair R. of it.
Small footstool in front of table.
Cloth on table.
Basket of laundry including: a pair of bloomers made in two halves and joined by poppers, large hole in back of bloomers.

In ORCHESTRA PIT

Broken drum, very bent triangle and fambourine.

OFF R.

Feather duster	TWANKEY
Parcels	WISHEE

Scene Four

OFF R.

Block of ice (thin wire frame covered with cellophane)	PONG

OFF L.

Parcels, paper carrier bags, three packets of sugar (to collect and bring into Auditorium)	WISHEE

Scene Five

Check ring	ABANAZAR

Scene Six

Set on stage: Magic lamp on pedestal L. C. by steps.

OFF R.

Plate of sandwiches for the SLAVE OF THE LAMP to produce.

PART TWO

Scene Seven

Set on stage: Bench (large enough to seat five) in front of washing machines.

Behind washing machines: large prop glue pot marked "GLUE", pair of dark glasses.

Card with "STADIRT".

Card with "BLAKANBLUINITE".

Inside Machine 2 cardboard replica of PONG's pants.

Inside Machine 3 cardboard replica of PING's vest.

Inside Machine 4 cardboard replica of EMPRESS's nightie.

Inside Machine 5 cardboard replica of TYPHOO's collar.

D.R. kitchen table: set of scales on U.S. end, till on D.S. end with a drawer which can be pushed through either the back or the front of it. (Drawer should be made longer than the till itself.) Telephone, large packet marked "WIFF", 10 soap cups on two trays with five on each.

Under table 7 washboards and soda syphon in laundry basket. Below table D.S. end large prop mangle.

In front of D.R. entrance large prop iron.

Launderette-type bags for CHORUS on bench.

OFF L.

Bundle of laundry to be thrown through window.

Laundry bag containing nightie and hanky	EMPRESS
Laundry bag with vest and shirt (made in two halves and joined by poppers)	PING
Laundry bag with pair of pants	PONG
Laundry bag with a pair of combinations with crest on seat	EMPEROR
Collar	TYPHOO
Coins	PING, PONG, EMPEROR & EMPRESS
Diamonds and lamp	ALADDIN

PERSONAL

TWANKEY	Whistle and thimbles.
WISHEE	Thimbles
PING & PONG	Thimbles
EMPEROR & EMPRESS	Thimbles
TYPHOO	Thimbles

Scene Eight

OFF R.

Double throne chair	PING & PONG

OFF L.

Jewels	ALADDIN
Trays of jewels	1st, 2nd, 3rd, 4th, 5th, 6th CHORUS
Check truncheon	PONG
Check lamp	ALADDIN

Scene Nine

OFF L.

Crystal Ball	ABANAZAR

Scene Ten

OFF L.

Upright chair	PING
Bench	PING & PONG

Check PING's whistle

Little green flag	PING
Cut-out of steam engine. Trolley with prop Espresso machine with three handles – one made to break off. Two soda syphons concealed in machine with rubber tubing running to L. and R. and angled to squirt upwards. Cup and saucer on machine and concealed half pint glass and jug of beer.	PONG
Plate of rock cakes	PING
Plate of Christmas pudding (covered ball)	PONG
Music sheets	PING & PONG

OFF R.

Plate of sausage rolls, one of which disguises a small pistol (loaded)	PONG
Check lamp	ALADDIN
Tray of lamps	ABANAZAR

PERSONAL

TWANKEY   Reticule containing small loaded starter's pistol.

Scene Eleven

If tabs are used set on stage notice board at C. "DESIRABLE BUILDING SITE FOR SALE".

Set in ORCHESTRA PIT

Pyjama cord.

OFF L.

Pyjama trousers with music written on them.
Prop pyjama jacket to match with song sheet words on it.   TYPHOO

OFF R.

Check ring   ALADDIN

Scene Twelve

Set on stage: Couch L.C. Table beside couch with five goblets on it.
                  Check lamp ABANAZAR.

OFF R.

Hook-on beards   ALADDIN &
                                                              WISHEE

Rope   CAMEL

Large gold jug   ABANAZAR

Phial of poison   ALADDIN

Scene Thirteen

OFF L.

PING's scooter   TYPHOO

OFF R.

PONG's scooter   CAMEL

EFFECTS PLOT

PAR' ONE

Scene One

1.	Police siren	Off R.
2.	Police siren	Off L.
3.	Glass crash, (bucket of broken glass thrown into a second bucket)	Off L.
4.	Motor engine	Grams.
5.	Backfiring, (blank pistol)	Off R.
6.	Loud crash	Off R.
7.	Motor engine	Grams.
8.	Backfiring	Off R.
9.	Loud crash	Off L.

Scene Two

10.	Thunder roll (thunder sheet)	Off, as convenient
11.	Thunder roll	Off, as convenient

| 12. | Thunder roll | Off, as convenient |
| 13. | Thunder roll | Off, as convenient |

Scene Three

14.	Tambourine crash	Off L.
15.	Door knock	Off D. L.
16.	Loud door knock	Off D. L.
17.	Loud door knock	Off U. R.
18.	Loud door knock	Off D. R.
19.	Loud door knock	Off D. L.
20.	Loud door knock	Off U. R.
21.	Loud door knock	Off D. R.
22.	Loud door knock	Off D. L.
23.	Telephone bell	Off U. C.
24.	Loud door knocks	Off D. L., U. R., D. R.

Scene Five

25.	Crack of thunder	Off, as convenient
26.	Heavy rumbling sound of cave opening	Off R.
27.	Thunder rolls	Off, as convenient

Scene Six

28.	Crash of thunder	Off, as convenient
29.	Heavy rumbling of cave closing	Off R.
30.	Thunder rolls	Off, as convenient
31.	Thunder rolls	Off, as convenient

PART TWO

Scene Seven

| 32. | Telephone bell | Off R. |
| 33. | Wind noise, (wind machine) | Off, as convenient |

Scene Ten

| 34. | Thunder | Off, as convenient |
| 35. | Wind noise | Off, as convenient |

Scene Eleven

| 36. | Thunder | Off, as convenient |
| 37. | Wind noise | Off, as convenient |

Scene Twelve

| 38. | Thunder | Off, as convenient |
| 39. | Wind noise | Off, as convenient |

MUSIC PLOT

PART ONE

1.   Overture

Scene One

2.	Opening Chorus, "CHING-A-LING"	CHORUS
3.	Ping's entrance music	ORCHESTRA
4.	"IN OLD PEKIN"	PING & PONG
5.	Aladdin's entrance music	ORCHESTRA
6.	"WHILE THERE'S LIFE"	ALADDIN & CHORUS
7.	Typhoo's entrance music	ORCHESTRA
8.	Chinese march	ORCHESTRA
9.	Twankey's entrance music	ORCHESTRA
10.	"SIXTY GLORIOUS YEARS"	TWANKEY
11.	"MAKE WAY"	PING, PONG & CHORUS
12.	"HAS ANYBODY SEEN MY HEART?"	ALADDIN & BALDROUBADOUR
13.	"CANTATA" (continue, orchestra only as link to next scene)	ENSEMBLE

Scene Two

14.	Abanazar's music	ORCHESTRA
15.	Slave of Ring's music	ORCHESTRA
16.	Abanazar's music, reprise 14.	ORCHESTRA
17.	Ping and Pong's music, reprise 4. (continue as link to next scene)	ORCHESTRA

Scene Three

18.	Typhoo's music, reprise 7.	ORCHESTRA
19.	"LET'S GO DREAMING"	ALADDIN and BALDROUBADOUR
20.	Chase music	ORCHESTRA
21.	Chase music, reprise 20	ORCHESTRA

22.	Comic fight music	ORCHESTRA
23.	Comic fight music	ORCHESTRA
24.	Chase music, reprise 20, as link to next scene	ORCHESTRA

Scene Four

25.	"SHOPPING"	WISHEE
26.	Mysterioso music as link to next scene	ORCHESTRA

Scene Five

27.	Abanazar's music, reprise 14	ORCHESTRA
28.	Link to next scene	ORCHESTRA

Scene Six

29.	Abanazar's music, reprise 14	ORCHESTRA
30.	Slave of Lamp's music	ORCHESTRA
31.	Music shimmer	ORCHESTRA
32.	Ballet	SLAVE OF LAMP and CHORUS
33.	Slave of Lamp's music, reprise 30	ORCHESTRA

PART TWO

34.	Entr'acte.	

Scene Seven

35.	"WIDOW TWANKEY'S LAUNDERETTE"	CHORUS
36.	Washing machine music	ORCHESTRA
37.	Washing machine music	ORCHESTRA
38.	"WASHBOARD BLUES"	TWANKEY, PING, PONG, WISHEE, EMPEROR, EMPRESS and TYPHOO
39.	Slave of Lamp's music, reprise 30	ORCHESTRA
40.	"HAS ANYBODY SEEN MY HEART", reprise 12	ALADDIN and BALDROUBADOUR
41.	Chinese march, reprise 8, as link to next scene	ORCHESTRA

Scene Eight

42.	Chinese fanfare	ORCHESTRA
43.	Slave Girl's music	ORCHESTRA
44.	Slave Girl's music, reprise 43	ORCHESTRA
45.	Slave Girl's music, reprise 43	ORCHESTRA

46.	Slave Girl's music, reprise 43	ORCHESTRA
47.	Slave Girl's music, reprise 43	ORCHESTRA
48.	"EMPEROR'S SONG"	EMPEROR
49.	Abanazar's music, reprise 14, as link to next scene	ORCHESTRA

Scene Nine

| 50. | Chinese march, reprise 8, as link to next scene | ORCHESTRA |

Scene Ten

51.	Chinese fanfare, reprise 42	ORCHESTRA
52.	"SING A SONG OF SIXPENCE"	ENSEMBLE
53.	"RECIPE"	TWANKEY and BALDROUBADOUR
54.	Slave of Lamp's music, reprise 30	ORCHESTRA
55.	Link to next scene	ORCHESTRA

Scene Eleven

56.	"PANDA PUZZLE"	TWANKEY, TYPHOO and AUDIENCE
57.	Slave of Ring's music, reprise 15	ORCHESTRA
58.	Link to next scene	ORCHESTRA

Scene Twelve

59.	Eastern dance	CHORUS
60.	"CONSTANT LOVE"	BALDROUBADOUR
61.	Camel's music	ORCHESTRA
62.	Comic eastern dance	ALADDIN, WISHEE, TWANKEY
63.	Slave of Lamp's music, reprise 30	ORCHESTRA
64.	Reprise 4, "IN OLD PEKIN" as link to next scene.	ORCHESTRA

Scene Thirteen

| 65. | "LOST" | PING, PONG, CAMEL and TYPHOO |
| 66. | "MAKE WAY", reprise 11 (Continue, orchestra only, for walk-down.) | CHORUS |

Scene Fourteen

| 67. | Fanfare | ORCHESTRA |
| 68. | Finale, "MAKE WAY", reprise 11 | TUTTI |